新装版
パーフェクト攻略
IELTS
［編著］
トフルゼミナール

リーディング

PERFECT STRATEGIES
FOR READING SECTION

テイエス企画

はじめに

日本で英語運用能力試験というと、まず英検とTOEICを思い浮かべる人が多いのではないでしょうか。海外大学への留学を目指す人にとってはTOEFLもなじみがあるかもしれません。しかし、近年IELTS（International English Language Testing System）に関心が集まっています。2000年以降全世界で受験者が急増し、今では年間300万人以上となっています。

これまで、IELTSというとイギリスやオーストラリアの大学への留学を希望する学生が受ける試験との印象が強かったかもしれませんが、今や多くの米国大学でも学生の英語運用能力の判断基準として導入されています。日本では大学のみならず、政府機関も国家公務員試験にIELTSを採用する傾向があります。これからも実用的な英語力を正確に測定できる試験としてIELTSはさらに身近なものになるでしょう。

IELTSのリーディングセクションの試験には、他の英語検定試験と異なる点があります。まず、解答用紙はマークシートではなく、すべて記述式となっています。そして、問題形式が多様です。文章の内容を表にまとめたり、要約を完成させたり、見出しを選んだりしなければなりませんので、選択肢形式の画一化された問題とは異なり受験者の幅広い対応力が試されます。

本書では、まず例題を解きながらリーディングセクションのすべての設問形式の分析と解法の確認をします。その後、本試験4回分の演習問題で徹底的に読んで解く訓練をします。さまざまな設問形式がランダムに登場しますので、苦手な形式をなくしましょう。最後に、総仕上げとして本試験と同じ形式と分量の模試に取り組みます。

この一冊を解ききり、リストアップされた重要語句を繰り返し復習すれば、IELTS試験のリーディングセクションの対策は万全です。本書が皆さんの国際舞台での活躍の足がかりになることを願っています。

トフルゼミナール

目　次

本書の取り組み方

◆ **本書の構成**

第1章　知っておきたい11の設問タイプ

リーディングセクションで扱われる設問のタイプを11に分けて紹介します。例題を解きながら、問題の特徴や何を問われているのかについて確認しましょう。

第2章　リーディングセクション問題演習

さまざまな分野の問題で実力を養成します。各問題には第1章で学んだ設問タイプが盛り込まれていますので、各設問タイプの解法に習熟するよう取り組んでください。解答解説では、問題に登場した重要単語をリストアップしていますので、復習の際にはこれらを覚えて語彙力を高める努力をするとスコアアップにつながります。各分野の英文は興味深いテーマが揃っていますので、味わいながら何度も読み返すことで、読解力をゆるぎないものにしましょう。

第3章　リーディング実戦模試

本番同様、3つのパッセージにまとめて挑戦する実戦模試です。時間内にどれくらい問題を解けるか、また正しく読み取れているかを確認しましょう。

解答用紙　巻末には、Exerciseと実戦模試のための解答用紙があります。コピーを取るか、切り取ってそのまま使用することができます。

IELTSについて

❖ IELTSとは？

　IELTS（アイエルツ）は、International English Language Testing Systemの略称で、ブリティッシュ・カウンシル、IDP：IELTS オーストラリア、ケンブリッジ大学ESOLが共同運営、管理する英語力判定試験です。世界140カ国で実施されており、年間約300万人が受験しています。16歳以上であれば、誰でも受験することができ、TOEFL（アメリカの非営利テスト開発機関ETSによって運営、管理されている留学時に提出できる英語資格試験の1つ）と同様に海外留学や研修の際に自分の英語力を証明するためのスコアとして利用することができます。

　試験はGeneral Training Module（一般英語）とAcademic Module（学術英語）に分かれており、受験者の目的によってどちらを受けるかを決める必要があります。Academic ModuleはGeneral Training Moduleよりも難易度が高く、海外の高等教育機関への提出用のスコアとして利用できます。ただし、リスニングセクションとスピーキングセクションの試験内容は共通です。本書はAcademic Moduleのリーディングセクション対策本です。

❖ IELTSの構成（Academic Moduleの場合）

科目	試験時間	内容
Listening	30分	4セクション・40問
Reading	60分	長文3題・40問
Writing	60分	2題
Speaking*	11分〜14分	3パート・質問数不定

*Speakingはネイティブスピーカーとのインタビュー形式

❖ IELTSのスコア

　IELTSのテスト結果は受験日から約2週間で発行されます。スコアはバンドスコア（Band Score）と呼ばれる1.0〜9.0までの0.5刻みの評価数値で表されます。1.0は英語の運用能力はほとんどない初級レベルで、9.0はネイティブスピーカーに近い運用能力を持つことを意味します。各科目のバンドスコアと、すべての合計を平均した総合バンドスコアが通知されます。発行後の有効期限は2年間です。

バンドスコア一覧

Band		レベル
9	Expert User	十分な運用能力があり、適切で正確な表現を用いることができる。
8	Very Good User	十分な運用能力があるが、不得意な分野では間違いや、ぎこちない表現が散見される。
7	Good User	内容によっては誤解している場合もあるが、おおむね正確に理解し、複雑な表現も用いることができる。
6	Competent User	内容によっては誤解している場合もあるが、おおむね正確に理解し、得意分野では複雑な表現を用いることができる。
5	Modest User	部分的には実用的な表現力、理解力を持っており、おおむね正しい理解ができているが、間違いが散見される。
4	Limited User	慣れている状況や分野では基本的な運用能力がある。
3	Extremely limited User	限られた状況や分野では一定の運用能力がある。
2	Intermittent User	実質的なコミュニケーションが困難。
1	Non User	基本的な運用能力がない。

◆ 採点・評価について

　リーディングセクションの換算は毎回同じというわけではありません
が、おおよそ次の表のように換算されます。

素点	バンドスコア
39〜40点	9
37〜38点	8.5
35〜36点	8
33〜34点	7.5
30〜32点	7
27〜29点	6.5
23〜26点	6
19〜22点	5.5
15〜18点	5
13〜14点	4.5
10〜12点	4
8〜9点	3.5
6〜7点	3
4〜5点	2.5
3点	2
2点	1.5
1点	1

IELTS リーディングセクションについて

❖ リーディングセクションの特徴

　3つのパッセージが出題され、全部で40問です。パッセージの長さはそれぞれ異なり、3つ合わせて2,150〜2,750語です。地理、生物、歴史など多岐にわたる分野が出題され、大学生や大学院生向けの内容ですが、専門知識は必要ありません。人物名や地名など見慣れない固有名詞については必ず本文中に説明があります。もしくは、パッセージの終わりに単語や専門用語についての注釈がついています。文体はnarrative（物語文）、argumentative（論証文）など、通常、本やジャーナル誌、新聞で読むようなスタイルで書かれています。

　設問のタイプはさまざまですが、主な解答のしかたとして、答えを選択肢のリストから選ぶもの、または本文から抜き出すものがあります。本文から単語や数字を抜き出す際には、語数制限があります。解答は、全て記述式ですので、選択肢問題の場合でも、マークシートのように○を塗りつぶすのではなく、選択肢の記号（「A」や「B」など）を解答用紙の解答欄に記入します。

❖ IELTS リーディングセクション対策ポイント

1 1つのパッセージを20分以内で解く　　解答時間は60分で3パッセージ出題されるので、平均して1パッセージに20分かけて解く計算になります。しかし、パッセージによって難易度が異なりますし、得意・不得意な内容や文体があるはずです。1つのパッセージで20分を超えてしまう場合は、他のパッセージに取り組んでみて、そちらをまず解いてからもどるとよいでしょう。

2 パッセージを読んだ後に問題を読む　　IELTSの問題は、通常、According to paragraph 1, ...など、答えをどこから探せばよいのか示されていません。そのため、問題から読むのではなく、まずパッセージを読んで、それぞれの段落の内容を把握してから問題に挑むほうが効果的です。読みながらそれぞれの段落に自分なりの見出しをつけておくのもよい方法です。そうすれば問題を読んだ際に、おおよその段落を探せばよいのかすぐにわかるでしょう。

3 本文の流れにそって出題される傾向を手がかりにする　　設問のタイプにもよりますが、例えば選択肢問題の場合は、本文中、1問目の答えの根拠は2問目の答えの根拠の前に見つかるはずです。同様に2問目の答えの根拠は、3問目より前に

見つかります。これを知っていると、探す箇所が限られてくるので、効率よく問題を解くことができます。ただ、これはあくまでも傾向で、例外的なケースもあります。

4 選択肢中のパラフレーズを見つける 基本的に、パラフレーズに気づくことがとても重要です。多くの場合、本文中の具体的な描写は、正解となる選択肢では抽象的に表現されています。簡単な例で述べると、本文のJim played soccer and tennisは、正解となる選択肢ではJim played sportsと表現される、ということです。本文を読みながら情報を整理する際に、パラフレーズすると効果的です。

5 本文中の情報を使って問題を解く 予備知識を使って問題を解こうとしてはいけません。IELTSの問題は、全て本文の情報だけで解答が得られるようになっています。正誤問題には、TRUE, FALSE以外にNOT GIVENという少々厄介な選択肢があり、設問の情報について全く記述がない場合に選びます。したがって、予備知識で勝手に補ってTRUEやFALSEを選ばないように気を付けてください。本文から単語を抜き出す場合も必ず本文中から選んでください。必要な品詞に着目すると探しやすくなります。

6 指示文を確認する 設問の指示文を毎回しっかり読むことを勧めます。例えば、You may use any answer more than once（「同じ選択肢を何度も選んでよい」という指示）や、本文から単語や数字を抜き出して書く際の語数制限（NO MORE THAN TWO WORDS「2語以内」など）に注意してください。

7 解答用紙への記入に注意する 答えは全て記述式です。選択肢の文字のほか、単語や数字を書く場合もあります。字が読めなければ採点できませんので、綺麗に書くことを心掛けましょう。当然ながら、正しい綴りも大切です。また、解答は制限時間内に記入し終える必要があります。リスニングセクションのように、問題用紙から解答用紙に答えを転記する時間が別に設けられていないので注意してください。

8 普段からさまざまな英文を読む 勉強法としては、さまざまな文体の英文に触れることが必要です。読む際には、段落ごとに内容をまとめて、パラフレーズできるように訓練するとよいでしょう。

問い合わせ先

　受験申込み、受験料の支払いなどの手続きについては下記の問い合わせ先をご参照ください。(2020 年 2 月現在)

問い合わせ先①
公益財団法人 日本英語検定協会 IELTS 東京テストセンター
住所：〒162-8055 東京都新宿区横寺町 55
TEL：03-3266-6852
FAX：03-3266-6145
E-mail：jp500ielts@eiken.or.jp

問い合わせ先②
公益財団法人 日本英語検定協会 IELTS 大阪テストセンター
住所：〒530-0002 大阪市北区曽根崎新地 1-3-16 京富ビル 4F
TEL：06-6455-6286
FAX：06-6455-6287
E-mail：jp512ielts@eiken.or.jp

問い合わせ先③
一般財団法人 日本スタディ・アブロード・ファンデーション（JSAF）
住所：〒169-0075 東京都新宿区高田馬場 1-4-15 大樹生命高田馬場ビル 3F
TEL：03-6273-9356
FAX：03-6273-9357
E-mail：academic@japanstudyabroadfoundation.or.jp

インターネット問い合わせ先
公益財団法人 日本英語検定協会の運営する IELTS ホームページ
http://www.eiken.or.jp/ielts/
一般財団法人 日本スタディ・アブロード・ファンデーション（JSAF）のホームページ
http://www.jsaf-ieltsjapan.com
ブリティッシュ・カウンシルによる IELTS 紹介ページ
http://www.britishcouncil.jp/exam/ielts

知っておきたい
11の設問タイプ

Question Type 01 | 選択肢問題
Multiple Choice

⏰ **6 minutes**

*You should spend about 6 minutes on **Questions 1–2**, which is based on the reading passage below.*

The Ford Model T

At the start of the 20th century, few people travelled by automobile. Owning a car cost a small fortune, and driving was a complex task that required a specially trained chauffeur. Henry Ford planned to change all that by building a simple and reliable vehicle, to be known as the Model T, which would be affordable to the average American worker. To achieve this aim, he adapted the techniques of assembly line manufacture to the process of building automobiles. Before this time, cars were built by hand using teams of skilled workmen, which was a slow and expensive procedure. Ford's innovation was to place the unfinished car on a moving assembly line so that instead of the worker going to the car, the car came to the worker, who remained stationary and performed the same task over and over again. With this method, Ford was able to cut the assembly time of a complete car from twelve hours to less than six. This enabled him to regularly reduce the price of the iconic Model T and claim half of the total automobile market in the United States. The Model T was so successful that production continued for nearly 20 years, from 1908 to 1927.

Questions 1–2

Choose the correct letter, A, B, C or D.

1   The novelty in Henry Ford's method was to

   A   build a vehicle that any worker could afford.

   B   move the cars along the production line while the workers stayed in place.

   C   create the process of assembly line production.

   D   introduce teams of skilled workers in the factory to perform complex tasks.

2   Thanks to Henry Ford's innovation, his iconic car

   A   continued to be built for more than two decades.

   B   sold as many cars as all other car models combined.

   C   became cheaper as production continued.

   D   became famous as the most successful ever.

Question Type 01　選択肢問題の攻略法

■**問題形式** パッセージに対して複数の設問があり、各設問にA～D、A～E、A～Gの選択肢が与えられています。設問の問いに最も適切に答えている選択肢を選びます。

■**攻略法** このタイプの設問では、本文と無関係、または真逆の内容の選択肢など、はっきりと間違いだと見抜けるものをできるだけ早く見つけることが解答にたどり着くポイントになります。本文中の鍵となる文は、ほとんどの場合書き換えられていますから、表現の言い換えに注意して、正しい選択肢を選べるように練習しましょう。また、設問は文章の流れの順に出題されています。例えば2問目の設問は1問目で問われる本文内容よりも後のことを尋ねています。解答する際に、どこを読めばよいかの判断をする基準にしましょう。

■**実力強化のポイント** 本文の要旨を踏まえて不要な選択肢を見抜く力、設問文を補完する選択肢を選んで文を再構成する力、本文の言い換えを正しく理解する力などが求められます。

例題の解答・解説

正解　**1** B　**2** C

問題文全訳

6分間を目安にして、以下の問題文をもとに**設問1-2**に答えなさい。

フォードのモデル**T**

❶ 20世紀の初頭、自動車で移動する人はあまりいなかった。❷ 車を所有するにはちょっとしたお金がかかり、車を運転するのは複雑な作業で特別に訓練されたお抱え運転手が必要であった。❸ ヘンリー・フォードは、後にモデルTとして知られることになる、平均的なアメリカの労働者が購買可能となるような、単純な構造で安定した性能の乗り物を設計することにより、そうした状況すべてを変えようとした。❹ この目的を達成するため、彼は車の製造過程に流れ作業方式を取り入れた。❺ これ以前、車は熟練した作業員のチームを使って手作業で組み立てられていたが、ゆっくりでコストのかかる工程であった。❻ フォードの技術革新は、仕上がっていない車を動く組み立てラインに並べ、作業員が車の所へ行き作業するかわりに、車が作業員のところに行くようにする事により、作業員は動かないで同じ作業を繰り返すということにあった。❼ この方法によ

り、フォードは車を完成させる時間を12時間から6時間以下にまで短縮可能にした。❽これによって、彼はこの時代を象徴するモデルTの価格を定期的に下げ、アメリカの自動車市場の半分を占めることができるようになった。❾モデルTは非常に成功をおさめ、1908年から1927年の20年近くにわたり生産が続いた。

設問1-2

正しいものを**A**, **B**, **C**, **D**から選びなさい。

1 ヘンリー・フォードの斬新なやり方は
A どんな労働者にでも手頃に買える乗り物をつくることだった。
B 作業員を同じ場所にとどめて車を生産ライン上で動かすことだった。
C 組み立て生産ラインの工程を立案することだった。
D 複雑な作業を行なう熟練した作業員のチームを工場に動員させることだった。

2 ヘンリー・フォードの技術革新のおかげで、彼の象徴的な車は
A 20年以上製造を継続した。
B 他のモデルの車の合計と同じ台数を販売した。
C 製造を継続していく中でより安価になった。
D かつて無い成功により、有名になった。

解説

1 第6文で、ヘンリー・フォードの斬新な方法は作業員が車のもとへ行くのではなく、車が作業員の所に来ることにより生産性を上げるものであると述べられている。ここでのキーワードは innovation（技術革新）である。

2 第8文で、車の組み立て時間を半分以下に減らすことによって、フォードはモデルTの価格を下げたとある。市場の半分を占めることができたのはhim、つまりフォードの会社であってモデルTではないのでBは誤り。最終文によると、生産が続いたのはnearly 20 years（20年近く）なのでAも誤り。Dについてはthe most successful everとまで言える程の根拠が本文にない。

⏱ **6 minutes**

*You should spend about 6 minutes on **Questions 1–3**, which are based on the reading passage below.*

What does it mean to be 'smart'?

The concept of multiple intelligences did not become widely known until 1983, when Howard Gardner, an American developmental psychologist, introduced the idea in his book *Frames of Mind: The Theory of Multiple Intelligences*. Gardner claimed that traditional methods of measuring intelligence, such as IQ tests, cannot sufficiently explain cognitive ability. Since 1999, Gardner has identified eight intelligences: linguistic, logic-mathematical, musical, spatial, bodily/kinaesthetic, interpersonal, intrapersonal, and naturalistic.

Gardner's theory has had a profound influence on how intelligence is perceived and has fuelled debate over how school teachers should assess the cognitive abilities of their students. For instance, according to the theory, a child who learns to multiply easily is not necessarily more intelligent than a child who has more difficulty on this task. The child who needs more time to master multiplication may in fact learn to multiply effectively through an alternative approach or may excel in other fields unrelated to mathematics. It may also be possible that the child is attempting to understand the multiplication process at a deeper level, which can result in slowness and conceal a mathematical intelligence which is potentially higher than that of a child who simply memorises the multiplication table.

Questions 1–3

Do the following statements agree with the information given in the reading passage?

Write

TRUE *if the statement agrees with the information*

FALSE *if the statement contradicts the information*

NOT GIVEN *if there is no information on this*

1 Gardner suggested that IQ tests were of limited use in measuring a person's intelligence.

2 Today, everyone accepts Gardner's ideas about measuring the intellects of students.

3 Children who are initially good at multiplication tend to become better mathematicians.

Question Type 02　正誤問題①の攻略法

●問題形式 設問文が本文の情報と①一致する、②矛盾する、あるいは③本文から判断できない／書かれていない、という3通りの選択肢から判断して解答する記述式の問題。

●攻略法 本文を読む前に、問題文の表現・内容をできるだけ正確に理解しましょう。この設問タイプでは特にFALSEとNOT GIVENを正確に見極めることが重要になってきます。FALSEは本文と矛盾すること、NOT GIVENは本文に記述のないことがポイントです。本文上の情報以外の自分の知っていることなどは一切頼りにせずに答えましょう。

●実力強化のポイント 本文に書かれている特定の情報を正確に認識する力が求められます。

例題の解答・解説

正解 1 TRUE　2 FALSE　3 NOT GIVEN

問題文全訳

6分間を目安にして、以下の問題文をもとに**設問1–3**に答えなさい。

「賢い」とはどういうことなのか

1 ❶多重知能の概念は広く知られていなかったが、1983年にアメリカの発達心理学者のハワード・ガードナーが彼の著書 *Frames of Mind: The Theory of Multiple Intelligences* でこの概念を紹介した。❷ガードナーはIQテストなどの知能を測定するための従来の方法では認知能力を十分に明確にできないと主張した。❸1999年以来、ガードナーは8つの知能を特定した。それは言語知能、論理・数学的知能、音楽知能、空間的知能、身体・運動感覚知能、対人的知能、内省的知能、そして博物学的知能だ。

2 ❶ガードナーの理論は、知能の理解の仕方に深い影響を与え、学校の教師がどのように学生の認知能力を測定するべきかという議論も激化した。❷例えば、この理論によれば、掛け算を容易に学ぶ子供は、掛け算を覚えるのに苦労する子供より必ずしも知能が高いわけではない。❸掛け算を習得するのに時間を必要とする子供は、実は別の方法で覚えた方が効果的かもしれないし、他の分野において秀でているかもしれない。❹更に、その子供は掛け算をより深いレベルで理解しようとしていて、そのため時間がかかり、単に掛け算表を暗記した生徒より高い数学的知能があるかもしれないことを見えな

くしている可能性がある。

設問1–3

次の記述は本文の情報に一致するか。

情報に一致するなら、**TRUE** と書き、

情報に矛盾するなら、**FALSE** と書き、

情報がないなら、**NOT GIVEN** と書きなさい。

1 ガードナーは人の知能を測るのにIQテストはあまり有効ではないと示唆した。

2 今日、学生の知能の測定法についてのガードナーの考え方は万人に受け入れられている。

3 掛け算がもともと得意な子供は数学に長けた大人になる可能性が高い。

┃解説┃

1 1段落2文で、IQテストでは人の認知能力を十分に説明できないとガードナーの著書で主張されているとある。

2 2段落1文によると、ガードナーの理論は認知能力の捉え方を巡り論争をおこしている。従って万人に受け入れられているのではない。

3 3の内容についての記述は本文中のどこにも見当たらない。

⏰ **6 minutes**

*You should spend about 6 minutes on **Questions 1–3**, which are based on the reading passage below.*

The Polygraph

A polygraph, commonly known as a lie detector, measures and records the pulse, blood pressure, and respiration (among other physiological features) of a subject who is being asked a series of questions. When the subject gives a deceptive answer, it is believed that he or she will show physiological responses that are notably different from those associated with honest answers. These include increased heartbeat and blood pressure, as well as changes in breathing rhythm.

Over 90 years have passed since the invention of the polygraph, but it has not yet been accepted by the scientific, legal or political communities. There is good reason to be sceptical, however, since every once in a while serious criminals are able to beat the polygraph. In 2003, Gary Ridgway, a serial killer who murdered 49 women in Seattle, confessed to his crime. It is disturbing to know that Ridgway had passed a lie detector test in 1987, while another man—who turned out to be innocent—had failed. Some speculate that psychopaths like Ridgway are able to trick the polygraph because they have lower anxiety levels than ordinary people, but the research into this has been inconclusive.

Questions 1–3

Do the following statements agree with the claims of the writer given in the reading passage?

Write

YES   *if the statement agrees with the claims of the writer*

NO   *if the statement contradicts the claims of the writer*

NOT GIVEN *if it is impossible to say what the writer thinks about this*

1   The scientific community has acknowledged the usefulness of polygraphs.

2   Ridgway confessed to his crime because he wanted to prove that he was able to beat a polygraph.

3   Using a polygraph could lead to wrongful convictions of innocent people.

Question Type 03　正誤問題②の攻略法

■**●問題形式**　設問文が本文の筆者の主張と①一致する、②矛盾する、あるい
は③本文から判断できない／書かれていない、という3通りの選択肢から判
断して解答する記述式の問題。
■**●攻略法**　文を読む前に、問題文の表現・内容をできるだけ正確に理解しま
しょう。正誤問題①と同様にNOとNOT GIVENを正確に見極めることが重
要になってきます。NOは筆者の主張と矛盾すること、NOT GIVENは筆者の
意見として言及されてないことがポイントです。本文上の情報以外の自分の
知っていることなどは一切頼りにせずに答えましょう。
■**●実力強化のポイント**　本文に書かれている特定の意見やアイデアについて正
確に認識する力が求められます。

▌例題の解答・解説

|正解|　**1 NO　2 NOT GIVEN　3 YES**
|問題文全訳|
6分間を目安にして、以下の問題文をもとに**設問1-3**に答えなさい。

ポリグラフ

1　❶一般的にうそ発見器と呼ばれているポリグラフは、いくつかの質問をされている
被験者の脈、血圧、呼吸（そして他の生理的特徴）を測定し、記録する。❷被験者が答
えを誤魔化そうとすると、正直に答える時に比べて、著しく異なる生理的反応をすると
信じられている。❸例えば、心拍数や血圧が上がり呼吸のリズムも変わることなどだ。

2　❶最初のポリグラフが発明されてから90年以上経つが、科学界や法曹界や政界で
は未だに受け入れられていない。❷しかし、懐疑的になるだけのもっともな理由があ
る。なぜなら、時折、連続殺人犯がポリグラフを騙すことが出来るからだ。❸2003年
にギャリー・リッジウェイというシアトル州で49人の女性を殺害した連続殺人犯が自
分の犯行を自白した。❹リッジウェイは1987年にポリグラフのテストに「合格」して
いた一方、別の、実は無罪の男性が「不合格」だったことには不安を覚える。❺リッジ
ウェイのような精神病質者は普通の人間より不安度が低いため、ポリグラフを騙すこと
が出来ると推測する人もいるが、これに関する研究は結論に達していない。

設問1–3

次の記述は本文の筆者の主張に一致するか。

> 筆者の主張に一致する場合は、**YES**と書き、
> 筆者の主張に矛盾する場合は、**NO**と書き、
> 筆者がこれに関してどう考えているのか分からない時は、**NOT GIVEN**と書きなさい。

1 科学界はポリグラフの実用性を認めている。

2 リッジウェイは、ポリグラフを騙すことが出来たことを証明したくて、犯行を自白した。

3 ポリグラフを使うと、罪なき人々の不当な有罪判決につながる場合がある。

|| 解説 ||

1 2段落1文で、ポリグラフは科学界では未だ受け入れられていないとある。

2 リッジウェイがポリグラフを騙せることを証明したという記述は本文中に見当たらない。

3 2段落4文で、無実の男性がポリグラフのテストにパスしなかったとある。

⏰ **8 minutes**

You should spend about 8 minutes on **Questions 1–3**, *which are based on the reading passage below.*

Safe Driving

A The dangers associated with using cell phones when driving are well documented. In almost every country it is now illegal to drive while holding a phone. One exception is the United States, where some states allow the practice and others do not. Conventional wisdom sees hands-free phones as the safer alternative, and this seems to make intuitive sense. Now a new report has overturned this assumption.

B The report studied the level of distraction experienced by drivers while performing various tasks and found that using a hands-free device is just as dangerous as using one that has to be held. In a simulation involving 60 drivers, only four managed to pass a driving test while talking on a phone. Two of those who passed were using a handset and two were not. In fact, chatting on a phone while driving was found to be almost as dangerous as driving while drunk.

C The results suggest that cell phones are an additional hazard to the already dangerous practice of driving. When drivers need to concentrate on maintaining a conversation, their chances of becoming distracted are greatly increased. Drivers talking on a cell phone overlook up to half of what is going on around them, and the capacity of the brain in the area that processes moving images is reduced by nearly one-third.

D Interestingly, it was found that drivers who listened to the radio experienced little distraction, and traffic psychologists have even suggested that it could have positive effects. Music helps drivers to focus, particularly on long, monotonous journeys, without interfering with their ability to 'tune back in' mentally when they encounter situations that require them to concentrate. It is difficult for drivers to adapt in this way when talking on the phone.

Questions 1–3

The reading passage has four paragraphs, **A–D**.

Which paragraph contains the following information?

*Write the correct letter, **A–D**.*

1   a description of how participating in a conversation while driving affects our mental processes

2   an example of an acceptable form of activity for drivers on tedious journeys

3   a comparison of driving while talking on a cell phone with an activity known to be dangerous

■**問題形式** 各段落にアルファベットが示されており、設問文の内容を含んでいる段落を答える選択式の問題。

■**攻略法** 段落内の特定の情報をできるだけ早く限定することが重要です。設問文で言い換えられた表現や要約された情報を本文から見つけ出すためには、各段落の要旨をある程度理解した上で解答すると該当箇所を見つけやすくなるでしょう。また、同じ段落が複数の設問の正解となる場合もあるので注意しましょう。

■**実力強化のポイント** 各段落の特定の情報を素早く理解し設問文とマッチングさせる力が求められます。

例題の解答・解説

|正解| 1 C　2 D　3 B
|問題文全訳|
8分間を目安にして、以下の問題文をもとに**設問1–3**に答えなさい。

安全運転

A　❶運転中の携帯電話の使用に危険が伴うことは十分に立証されている。❷今やほとんどの国で、携帯電話を手に持って運転することは違法である。❸例外はアメリカで、この慣習が認められている州とそうでない州がある。❹社会通念によればハンズフリーの携帯電話が安全な選択肢であり、こうした見方が直感的に納得できるように思われる。❺今では、ある新たな研究によってこの前提はくつがえされている。

B　❶その研究で運転手が様々な作業を行なっている間にどの程度注意がそれるのか調査したところ、ハンドフリー携帯の使用は手に持たなければならない携帯電話の使用と同様に危険であることがわかった。❷60人の運転手による模擬実験では、電話で話しながらの運転免許試験に何とか合格できたのはわずか4人だけだった。❸そのうちの2人は受話器型の携帯電話を使い、もう2人はワイアレスの使用だった。❹実際、運転中にしゃべることは飲酒運転と同じくらい危険である。

C　❶以上の調査結果は、携帯電話は車の運転という既に危険な行為をさらに危険にするものだと指摘している。❷運転手が会話の継続に集中する必要がある時、注意が

それる確率が非常に高くなる。❸携帯電話で話している運転手は周囲の出来事の半分程を見逃し、動きのある映像を処理する脳の部位の機能はほぼ3分の1減少する。

D ❶興味深い事に、ラジオを聞いていた運転手が注意をそらされることはほとんどないと分かり、交通心理学者はこのことには好ましい影響があるという指摘もしている。❷音楽は、とりわけ単調な長旅で運転手の集中力を促進させ、集中すべき状況に直面したときに意識を「集中モードに戻す」能力の妨げになることもない。❸電話で話している時は運転手がこのようなかたちで適応することは難しい。

設問1–3

本文には**A–D**の4つの段落がある。

下記の情報はどの段落に述べられているか。

A–Dの正しい文字を記入しなさい。

1 運転中に会話することがどのように知的機能に影響するかという説明
2 単調な旅において容認できる運転手の活動例
3 運転中の携帯電話の使用と危険だと知られている活動の比較

解説

1 C段落で、運転中の会話がどのように脳の機能に影響するか説明されている。

2 D段落で、単調な長旅の間に音楽を聞くことが運転に集中するのに役立つと指摘されている。

3 B段落最終文で、電話で話しながら運転することが飲酒運転と比較されている。

⏰ **8 minutes**

*You should spend about 8 minutes on **Questions 1–3**, which are based on the reading passage below.*

Questions 1–3

The reading passage has four paragraphs, **A–D**.

*Choose the correct heading for paragraphs **B–D** from the list below.*

	List of Headings
i	The historical development of irrational behaviour
ii	Creating an illusion of cause and effect
iii	Superstitious behaviour among non-humans
iv	The pervasiveness of irrational belief
v	One psychologist's strange superstitions
vi	The practical element in superstitious behaviour

Example	*Answer*
Paragraph **A**	**iv**

1   Paragraph **B**
2   Paragraph **C**
3   Paragraph **D**

The Meaning of Superstitious Behaviour

A　A superstition is the belief that certain behaviours or events can influence or bring about future events. Such beliefs are common throughout the world but vary widely from culture to culture. For example, many people in western societies consider the number thirteen to be unlucky while in Japan the same notion applies to the number four. People who avoid such numbers might think themselves rational yet still observe the superstition, suggesting an underlying belief in a causal relationship between an action or object and a certain outcome.

B　Superstitious habits are not confined to humans. One famous psychologist demonstrated that pigeons are also prone to such behaviour. He conducted a famous experiment where he placed a pigeon in a cage with an automatic food dispenser that delivered a food pellet every 15 seconds. He discovered that the pigeon soon developed a certain type of behaviour, and when he repeated the experiment with different pigeons he found that each one developed a unique ritual. For instance, one pigeon would turn anti-clockwise three times before looking at the food basket while another would thrust its head into the top-left corner.

C　The psychologist's explanation for this strange behaviour is quite straightforward. The pigeon is not aware that the food is delivered regardless of its own behaviour and knows little about how a food dispenser works, so it moves around in the cage in a random manner until food appears. Then, in order to produce the same result, the pigeon thinks that it needs to repeat the action it made previously.

D　Similarly, humans perform their own superstitious acts in an attempt to gain control over events in their lives. Elite sports players, who need to maintain strict control over their physical movement, are especially prone to developing such routines. Tennis player Serena Williams bounces the ball five times before her first serve and twice before her second. Wade Boggs, a former baseball player, claimed he performed better if he ate chicken the night before a game. By performing these rituals the players are able to maintain their confidence, so it could be argued that there are good reasons to carry out superstitious acts after all.

Question Type 05　マッチング問題②（見出し）の攻略法

●問題形式 各段落にアルファベットが示されており、その段落の内容に合う、適切な見出しを「List of Headings」から選び、見出しに付けられたローマ数字で答える記号選択式の問題。

●攻略法 このタイプの設問は必ず選択肢の内、一つを例として答えを示してくれているので、始めに解答例に使用された見出しを消してしまうとよいでしょう。残りの見出しを確認して、それぞれ関係がありそうな段落を選びましょう。全文をしっかりと読むのではなく、見出しの表現の言い換えや、前の段落との繋がりから、どんな内容の段落かを素早く判断できるように練習してください。ローマ字のviとivなどの書き間違いには注意しましょう。

●実力強化のポイント 全体の主旨を理解した上で、各段落の要旨を正確に見抜く力が求められます。

例題の解答・解説

正解 1 iii　2 ii　3 vi

問題文全訳

本文には**A–D**の4つの段落がある。

8分間を目安にして、以下の問題文をもとに**設問1–3**に答えなさい。

設問1–3

B–Dの段落にふさわしい見出しを見出しのリストから選べ。

	見出しのリスト
i	不合理な行動の歴史的な発達
ii	原因と結果という幻想の創造
iii	人間以外の迷信的行動
iv	非合理的考えの普及
v	ある心理学者の不思議な迷信
vi	迷信的行動の効果的な側面

1 段落**B**
2 段落**C**
3 段落**D**

縁起をかつぐ行動の意味

A ❶迷信とは、ある行為や出来事が未来の出来事に影響したり未来に何かを引き起こしたりするのだと信じることである。❷こうした考えは世界共通であるが、文化間によりかなり多様である。❸例えば、西洋の社会では多くの人々が数字の13は不吉だと考えるが、日本では同じ考えが数字の4にあてはまる。❹こういった数字を避ける人々は自分自身が合理的だと思っているかもしれないが、やはりそれは迷信に従っており、行動や物事と特定の結末との間に何らかの因果関係があると無意識のうちに信じていることを示唆する。

B ❶迷信的な行動様式は人間だけに限定されるものではない。❷ある有名な心理学者は鳩もそのような行動をとる傾向がある事を立証した。❸彼は15秒毎に餌を運ぶ自動配膳機を取り付けたかごに鳩を入れる有名な実験を行った。❹彼は鳩がほどなくある種の行動を取るようになることを発見し、彼が別の鳩にも繰り返し実験したところ、それぞれの鳩が独特の儀式をするようになっていることに気づいた。❺例えば、ある鳩は餌かごを見る前に3回反時計回りし、別の鳩は左上の角に頭をぐいと押し付けるといったことだ。

C ❶こうした不思議な行動に対する心理学者の説明は究めて明快である。❷餌が自分自身の行動に関係なく運ばれてくることや、配膳機がどのように作動するのか鳩は理解していないので、餌が現れるまで無作為に動き回る。❸それから、餌があらわれるという同じ結果を生み出すために、以前にした行動を繰り返す必要があると考えるのだ。

D ❶同様に、人間は自分の人生における出来事をコントロールしようと試みて自ら縁起をかつぐ行動をとる。❷身体の動きを厳密に管理し続ける必要のある一流スポーツ選手は特にそうしたルーティーンをする傾向がある。❸テニス・プレイヤーのセリーナ・ウィリアムズは最初のサーブの前にボールを5回バウンドさせ、2回目のサーブの前には2回バウンドさせる。❹元野球選手のウェイド・ボッグスは試合の

前の晩に鶏肉を食べた方が調子が出ると主張していた。❺こうした儀式を行うことで選手たちは自信を維持することができるので、やはり迷信的な行動を遂行するもっともな理由があると言えるだろう。

|解説|

1　B段落1文に迷信的習慣は人間だけに限らないとある。

2　C段落で、鳩の実験結果について根拠のない因果関係が作り出されているという説明が提示されている。

3　D段落で、迷信的な行動をとることによりスポーツ選手が自信を維持する例が挙げられている。

⏰ **6 minutes**

*You should spend about 6 minutes on **Questions 1–3**, which are based on the reading passage below.*

Theories of Language Acquisition

In the 1950s, B.F. Skinner provided one of the earliest explanations of language acquisition. As a pioneer in the science of behaviourism, which posits that behaviour is shaped by external influences, he suggested children learn languages through practice by associating words with meanings. When a child utters a word or grammatical structure correctly, the adult will smile or in other ways positively reinforce the sense of meaning. Skinner's theory became influential, but Noam Chomsky later suggested another idea. Chomsky's theory of universal grammar proposes that humans have an innate predisposition to put words into categories, such as nouns and verbs. It is this inborn ability that facilitates the child's development of language.

In his 1994 book *The Language Instinct*, Steven Pinker took this idea one step further by arguing that humans are born with a natural ability, like an instinct, to pick up language. He compares language to other species' specialised adaptations such as a spider's instinct to weave a web. As evidence for the universality of language, Pinker cites children who spontaneously invent a consistent grammatical speech (a creole) of their own if they grow up in a mixed-culture with no unifying influence.

A decade or so later, Geoffrey Sampson challenged the existence of universal grammar, arguing that a human baby is unlikely to be born with the ability to separate symbols into categories like nouns and verbs, and also rejected the notion of a language instinct, saying that Pinker's logic and facts were often incorrect. Sampson analysed a large body of data and concluded that children were good at learning languages simply because they were good at learning anything that they encountered, not because they had an in-built knowledge of language structures.

Questions 1–3

*Match each statement with the correct author, **A**, **B**, **C** or **D**.*

1 Human beings are born with an aptitude to divide words into a group according to their specific functions.
2 Children learn to use language by responding to praise when it is used accurately.
3 The ability of children to learn a language is no different from their ability to learn other things.

List of Authors

A   B.F. Skinner
B   Noam Chomsky
C   Steven Pinker
D   Geoffrey Sampson

Question Type 06　マッチング問題③（内容）の攻略法

●**問題形式**　本文で説明されている理論や概念についての設問文が複数提示され、その内容と一致する選択肢を複数の選択肢から選び出す記号選択式の問題。Type 1選択肢問題と違って、複数の設問について1つの選択肢グループが与えられる。

●**攻略法**　設問を確認して、抽象的な概念や理論についての説明を本文中でしっかり読みましょう。1つの段落の中に複数のキーワードが混在する場合もあるので、メインテーマだけを見て読み飛ばさないように注意してください。また、選択肢が複数回正解として使用される場合もあるので設問をよく読んで解きましょう。

●**実力強化のポイント**　文で説明されている意見・理論について正しく理解して、内容と関係がある選択肢を選び出す力が求められます。

例題の解答・解説

|正解|　**1** B　**2** A　**3** D
|問題文全訳|
6分間を目安にして、以下の問題文をもとに**設問1–3**に答えなさい。

言語習得の理論

1　❶1950年代にB.F.スキナーは言語習得についての最初期の見解の1つを提示した。❷行動は外的影響により形成されると仮定する行動主義の科学者の草分けの1人として、子どもは言葉と意味を結びつけて考える練習を通して言語を学ぶのだと彼は主張した。❸子どもが言葉や文法的な構造を正しく表現するとき、大人は微笑みや他の方法で積極的に言葉の意味を強化する。❹スキナーの理論は影響力が強くなったが、ノーム・チョムスキーが後に別の見解を示唆した。❺チョムスキーの普遍文法の理論は、人間は単語を名詞や動詞といったカテゴリーに分類する生得的な性質があるのだと提唱している。❻子どもの言語の発達を促進するのがこの生得的能力である。

2　❶1994年の著書「言語を生み出す本能」の中で、スティーブン・ピンカーはこの考えをさらに一歩推し進め、人間は本能と同様に言語を習得する生得的能力があると議論した。❷彼は、クモが巣をかける本能のような、他の種の特別な適応性と言語とを比較している。❸言語の普遍性の根拠として、ピンカーは統一的な影響力のない混合文化

第1章 設問TYPE

の中で育った場合、子どもたちが自ら文法的に一貫した発話（クレオール）を自発的に作り出すことを挙げている。

3 ❶それから10年ほど後に、ジェフリー・サンプソンが普遍文法の存在について異議を唱え、人間の赤ん坊は文字を名詞や動詞のようなカテゴリーにわける能力を備えていそうもないと論じ、さらにはピンカーの論理と事実は不正確である事が多いとして、言語習得本能という概念をも否定した。❷サンプソンは大量のデータを分析し、子どもが言語の学習に長けているのは単に遭遇する物事なら何でも習得するのが得意なだけであり、生得的な言語構造の知識を持っているわけではないのだと結論づけた。

設問1–3
それぞれの理論に合う適切な著者を*A, B, C, D*から選びなさい。

1 人間は特定の機能ごとに言葉をグループ分けする能力が生まれつき備わっている。
2 子どもは言葉を正確に使った時にほめられる事に反応して言語の使い方を学ぶ。
3 子どもの言語を学ぶ能力は他のことを学ぶ能力と何ら違いがない。

> **著者のリスト**
> **A** B.F. スキナー
> **B** ノーム・チョムスキー
> **C** スティーブン・ピンカー
> **D** ジェフリー・サンプソン

| 解説 |

1 1段落目の第5文以降で、ノーム・チョムスキーの理論として子どもの生得的能力について述べられている。

2 1段落目の第3文で、スキナーの理論に関して子どもが正しく発話した時の大人の反応について述べられている。

3 3段落目では、ジェフリー・サンプソンによる生得的な能力に対する反論が述べられている。

🕐 **6 minutes**

*You should spend about 6 minutes on **Questions 1–3**, which are based on the reading passage below.*

Dolphin Communication

Dolphins are social animals unique in their ability to convey meaning through a wide range of auditory and visual means. Auditory signals can take the form of whistles used to convey general meanings of excitement, happiness or panic. Family groupings also seem to produce sounds unique to each pod, and scientists studying bottlenose dolphins have found that individual dolphins develop a 'signature whistle' in infancy that identifies that dolphin and remains stable throughout its life. As well as whistles, dolphins produce pulsed sounds, known as clicks, that seem to be used mostly for echolocation purposes. Echolocation enables the dolphin to see the world through sound and create a mental image of the objects and spaces around it.

Nonverbal forms of communication include tail slapping and synchronous behaviour. Dolphins often hit the surface of the water with their tails, producing a booming sound that carries through water for long distances. A tail slap is frequently a signal of aggression, but it could also be a warning or simply a way of communicating, in the dolphin equivalent of a human wave, with friends swimming some distance away. Synchronous behaviour with other dolphins is thought to be a way of demonstrating close partnerships. It can also help when dolphins are threatened by a shark or other predator, giving the dolphins the chance to mount a coordinated defence.

Questions 1–3

*Complete each sentence with the correct ending, **A–E**, below.*

1   Unlike other animals, dolphins have the ability to

2   When dolphins drift away from other members of their group, they may

3   Dolphins that are threatened by a predator will tend to

A	synchronise their movements so as to improve their probability of survival.
B	slap their tails in the water as a warning.
C	communicate using a vast array of auditory signals.
D	use whistles to indicate anger to other pod members.
E	slap their tails in the water in order to gain attention.

> ●**問題形式** 設問文が未完成の状態で提示され、その後に続く文を選ぶ記号
> 選択式の問題。
> ●**攻略法** 不完全な状態の設問文を読み、キーワードから関連する文を本文
> から見つけ出しましょう。また設問は文章の流れの順に出題されています。
> 例えば2問目の設問は1問目で問われる本文内容よりも後のことを尋ねてい
> ます。解答する際に、どこを読めばよいかの判断をする基準にしましょう。
> ●**実力強化のポイント** 文の要旨を踏まえて不要な選択肢を見抜く力、欠けて
> いる情報を補完して文を再構成する力、本文の言い換えを正しく理解できる
> 力などが求められます。

例題の解答・解説

正解 1 C　2 E　3 A
問題文全訳

6分間を目安にして、以下の問題文をもとに**設問1–3**に答えなさい。

イルカのコミュニケーション

1 ❶イルカは幅広い聴覚的・視覚的な手段で意味を伝える能力を持つという点でユニークな社会性動物である。❷聴覚信号は、興奮や喜びや恐怖といった大まかな意味を伝えるのに使われるホイッスル音の形態をとっている。❸また、家族集団はそれぞれの群れで独特な音を作り出していると思われ、バンドウイルカを研究している科学者は、個々のイルカが自らを特定し生涯を通して変わらない「シグネチャー・ホイッスル」を幼い時期に発達させることを突き止めた。❹ホイッスルと同様にイルカはクリック音として知られるパルス音を作り出すが、大抵それは反響定位を目的に使われるようである。❺反響定位でイルカは音を通して外界を見て、身の回りにある空間や物体のイメージを頭の中で作ることができる。

2 ❶言語を使わない形態のコミュニケーションには、尾で水面を叩く行為や同期動作がある。❷イルカはよく、尾で水面を叩いたり長距離に轟きわたる音を出したりする。❸尾で水面を叩くのはしばしば敵意の兆候であるが、それは警告や単に遠く離れて泳いでいる友達へのコミュニケーションの方法の1つで、人が手を振る行為に相当する場合もある。❹他のイルカとの同期動作は緊密な関係の表現の1つであると考えられてい

る。❺また、イルカがサメやその他の捕食動物に脅かされている時にも役立つことがあり、組織的な防御を開始する機会になる。

設問1-3

*A–E*のうち正しい選択肢を選び、それぞれの文章を完成させよ。

1　他の動物と異なり、イルカは＿＿＿＿＿能力を持っている。
2　イルカが同じ群れの仲間から遠ざかっているとき、彼らは＿＿＿＿＿ようだ。
3　捕食動物によって脅かされている時イルカは＿＿＿＿＿傾向がある。

> **A**　生存の確率を上げるために体の動きを一致させる
> **B**　警告として尾で水を叩く
> **C**　幅広い聴覚的信号を使ってコミュニケーションをとる
> **D**　ホイッスルを使って他の群れの仲間に敵意を表す
> **E**　注意を引くために尾で水を叩く

|解説|

1　1段落2文ではイルカがホイッスルという形態の聴覚的信号を使うことが述べられており、3文では自分のIDとなるよう特有な音を出すことができるとあるので、相当数の数の聴覚的信号が使用されていることが理解できる。

2　2段落3文で、尾で水面を叩くことは敵意を表す以外に、離れた仲間とコミュニケーションを取るためだと述べられている。人が手を振ることにも例えられているので、注意を引くための行為と考えるのが自然だ。

3　捕食動物によって脅かされた場合については2段落最終文で言及があり、Itが防御する際などに役立つとあるが、これは前文の主語のSynchronous behaviour（同期動作）のことである。同じ内容を言い換えているのはA。

⏰ **6 minutes**

*You should spend about 6 minutes on **Questions 1–3**, which is based on the reading passage below.*

Massive Online Open Courses

The demand for higher education seems endless, and universities, along with their fees, are growing relentlessly. In the last few decades, the resources of the Internet have been harnessed through distance learning in order to satisfy this demand for learning while keeping costs down. Now the invention of MOOCs, or Massive Online Open Courses, has boosted the popularity of net-based courses.

MOOCs are courses of study made available over the Internet without charge. Anyone wanting to take a MOOC simply logs on to the relevant website and starts studying. There are now around 5,000 MOOCs offered by more than 600 universities, and last year 40 million students signed up for them. In addition to traditional course materials, many MOOCs provide access to user forums that support community interaction among students, professors and teaching assistants. Nevertheless, students taking MOOCs receive less personal attention than those taking regular courses, and in some cases none at all.

The potential reach of MOOCs offers a great opportunity for the best professors to enhance their reputations. The most famous of them, who might teach a 20-person seminar once a month at an Ivy League university, could find themselves teaching 10,000 people—more than they could teach in person in their entire lives—in a single session. Whatever form MOOCs eventually take, their impact on higher education is likely to be huge.

Questions 1–3

Complete the sentence below.

*Choose **NO MORE THAN TWO WORDS** from the passage for each answer.*

1 As the need for university education increases, the universities keep raising their _____.

2 MOOCs often provide an opportunity for students to interact with their professors through _____.

3 Through MOOCs _____ of eminent professors could be bolstered.

Question Type 08　短文空所補充問題の攻略法

●**問題形式**　短い設問文が与えられ、本文の内容に沿う文となるように、本文中から指定されたワード数で空所に入る適切な語を選び補充する記述式の問題。

●**攻略法**　文を完成させるための表現は本文中にあります。語数も制限されるので、最初に確認しておきましょう。解答は文字を書き入れるため、スペリングのミスなどないように本文中の語句と照らし合わせて注意しましょう。数字が解答に含まれる場合は、英字またはアラビア数字のどちらで書いてもよいです。

●**実力強化のポイント**　本文の特定の情報を見つけ出す力、設問文を補完する語や表現を問題の指示に従って選ぶ力などが求められます。

例題の解答・解説

正解　**1** fees　**2** user forums　**3** reputations

問題文全訳

6分間を目安にして、以下の問題文をもとに**設問1–3**に答えなさい。

大規模オンライン公開講座（**MOOC**）

1　❶高等教育の需要はとどまる事がないように思われるが、それに伴う学費は容赦なく上昇している。❷過去数10年間、コストを下げながらこの需要を満たすために通信教育でインターネットの力が利用されている。❸今やMOOC、すなわち、大規模オンライン講座の創設はインターネット講座の人気を押し上げている。

2　❶MOOCはインターネット上で無料で視聴可能となった教科課程である。❷MOOCを受講したければ誰でも関連するサイトにログオンするだけで、勉強を始められる。❸現在では5000近いMOOCが600以上の大学によって提供されていて、昨年は4000万人の学生が登録した。❹従来の講座用教材に加え、MOOCの多くは学生や教授、補助教員間のコミュニティーの交流を支える利用者用掲示板へのアクセスも提供している。❺それにもかかわらず、MOOCの受講生が正規の講座を受講している学生と比較して個人的な関心を持たれることは少なく、全く関心を持たれない場合もある。

3　❶MOOCの普及可能性は、質の高い教授陣に自らの評価を高める絶好の機会を提

供している。❷そうした教授達の中でも特に有名な人達は、名門大学で月に1回20人の
ゼミを受け持っているかもしれないが、気づいたらたった1回の授業で1万人という、
一生を通して教えうる以上の人達を教えている可能性も出てくる。❸MOOCがゆくゆ
くどんな形を取ろうとも、高等教育に対する影響は大きそうだ。

設問1-3

次の文を完成させよ。
それぞれ2語以内の言葉を文中から選んで解答しなさい。

1 大学教育の需要が増加するにつれ、大学は<u>授業料</u>を引き上げ続けている。
2 MOOCは学生が<u>利用者掲示板</u>を通して教授陣と交流する機会を提供し
 ている。
3 MOOCを通して著名な教授の<u>名声</u>は強化される。

|解説|

1 1段落1文に学費の高騰について述べられている。

2 2段落4文に、教授陣と交流する手段として利用者の掲示板について言及が
ある。

3 3段落1文にMOOCが教授陣の評判を高める機会を提供していることにつ
いて述べられている。

⏰ **8 minutes**

*You should spend about 8 minutes on **Questions 1–4**, which are based on the reading passage below.*

Sleep deprivation in the business world

Contemporary work culture celebrates sleep deprivation in the same way that cultures of previous generations admired those who could hold their drink. We certainly know that regularly sleeping for just four or five hours can produce effects similar to intoxication. Reaction speed, short- and long-term memory, the capacity to concentrate and the ability to make difficult decisions all start to suffer. The businessperson who regularly stays up all night (e.g. finishing notes for a presentation) is affecting their company's bottom line by performing below his or her peak, and sleep-deprived workers may contribute little despite being present at the company, thus creating the problem of 'presenteeism'.

One major factor that determines our ability to maintain cognitive performance at a high level has to do with the total amount of sleep we manage to get over several days. If we get at least eight hours of sleep a night, we are able to remain alert more or less constantly throughout the day, but if we manage on less than that for an extended period of time we build up a sleep deficit that makes it more difficult for the brain to function well. Another factor has to do with maintaining a circadian rhythm. Human beings evolved to stay awake during the day, not at night, so the businessperson who regularly takes the red-eye to Los Angeles for an 8 a.m. meeting is unlikely to be in a fit state to perform. To protect against sleep deficiency, companies should set out policies limiting scheduled work. For example, employees should not be allowed to put in more than 45 hours a week, even in exceptional circumstances.

Questions 1–4

*Complete the summary using the list of words, **A–I** below.*

We often praise people who work day and night without understanding the adverse effects that such practices can bring. In fact, **1** _____ sleep deprivation produces similar effects to being **2** _____, and while a worker may be sitting at his or her desk they may be unable to perform as in the case of **3** _____. In order to maintain concentration all day, we should sleep for eight hours out of twenty-four and maintain a regular **4** _____ rhythm. To help with this companies should limit employees' working hours.

A presenteeism	**B** drunk	**C** negative impact
D deficit	**E** stable	**F** chronic
G circadian	**H** short-term	**I** night-time

Question Type 09　要約・ノート・表・フローチャート完成問題の攻略法

●**問題形式** 欠落した部分を含む本文の要約文が与えられ、本文の内容に沿う文章となるように、本文中から指定されたワード数の語、または選択肢の記号で空所に入る適切な語を補充する記述式の問題。

●**攻略法** このタイプの設問では、チャートや図表、メモなど様々なフォーマットの文が扱われます。要約文を最初に読み、内容が結びつく箇所を的確に判断できるよう、英語で書かれている図面やメモのフォーマットに慣れておきましょう。語句を記述する場合はType 08と同様にスペリングミスには注意しましょう。

●**実力強化のポイント** 様々なパッセージのフォーマットに対応できる力、適切な語句を補充する文法力などが求められます。

例題の解答・解説

正解 1 F　2 B　3 A　4 G

問題文全訳

8分間を目安にして、以下の問題文をもとに**設問1–4**に答えなさい。

仕事場の睡眠不足

1 ❶現代の仕事文化は、今までの世代の文化が酒に強いことを称賛していたのと同様、睡眠不足を褒め称えている。❷定期的にたった4–5時間しか睡眠を取っていないと酒に酔った状態に似た効果が出ることがあると、はっきりと分かっている。❸反応速度、短期的・長期的な記憶、集中力や難しい決定を下す能力といった全てが悪化してくる。❹定期的に（例えばプレゼンテーションのメモ書きを書き終えるためなどで）徹夜をしている経営者は職務遂行能力がピークに至らないことにより収益に悪影響を及ぼし、睡眠不足の社員は会社にいながらほとんど貢献せず、こうして「プレゼンティーズム」という問題が引き起こされる。

2 ❶我々の認識能力を高水準で維持する能力を決定する重要な要因の1つは、数日間でとれる睡眠時間の合計時間と関連している。❷もし一晩につき少なくとも8時間の睡眠がとれるなら、大なり小なり1日を通して注意力を保っていられるが、もし8時間以下の睡眠で長期間やりくりしてしまうと、睡眠不足は慢性化し、脳が十分機能するのがより困難になる。❸もう1つの要因は概日リズムの維持と関連がある。❹人間は夜では

なく昼の間に目覚めたままでいるように進化したので、ロサンジェルスの朝8時のミーティングにいつも徹夜でくるようなビジネスマンは仕事をするのに適した状態とは言いがたい。❺睡眠不足を防ぐために、企業は所定労働時間を限定する企業方針を提示すべきである。❻例えば、たとえ例外的な状況下であっても、社員は週に45時間以上の就労を許容されるべきではない。

設問1-4

A-Iの選択肢を使って要約を完成させよ。

下記**A-I**の枠内の言葉を使って要約を完成しなさい。

私達は昼夜問わず休みなく働くという行為がもたらす悪影響を理解せずに、そのように働く人を褒めがちである。実際、慢性的な睡眠不足は酒に酔った状態と同様の影響をもたらし、プレゼンティーズムの場合は、従業員が自分の机に座っていても職務遂行能力が発揮できないかもしれない。集中力を一日中持続させるためには、24時間のうち8時間は睡眠をとるべきであり、規則正しい概日リズムを維持するべきである。これを支援するために企業は社員の就労時間を限定すべきである。

A プレゼンティーズム	**B** 酒に酔った	**C** 悪影響
D 不足	**E** 安定した	**F** 慢性の
G 24時間周期の	**H** 短期の	**I** 夜間の

|| 解説 ||

1　2段落2文で、長期にわたる睡眠不足は慢性化し、脳の動きを鈍らせるとある。

2　1段落2文で、睡眠不足は酒に酔った状態を引き起こすと述べられている。

3　1段落4文で、職務遂行能力の低下はプレゼンティーズムの状況であると述べている。

4　2段落3-4文で概日リズムを保つ必要性が示唆されている。

⏰ **6 minutes**

*You should spend about 6 minutes on **Questions 1–4**, which are based on the reading passage below.*

The Digestive System of a Cow

The cow's digestive tract comprises the mouth, oesophagus, a four-compartment stomach, small intestine and large intestine. The stomach includes the rumen, reticulum, omasum and abomasum. The rumen is the largest of the four compartments and is further divided into several sacs. Conditions inside the rumen are favourable for the growth of microbes, and the processes of digestion and fermentation take place here. The reticulum, located towards the front of the body cavity, resembles a pouch in appearance, and acts as a trap for any foreign objects that are ingested. The reticulum lies close to the heart, so the ingestion of sharp objects such as nails can prove fatal. The omasum is shaped like a sphere and acts as the gateway to the abomasum, absorbing water and other substances from the digestive contents. The function of the abomasum, which is sometimes called the 'true stomach,' is the chemical breakdown of food through hydrochloric acid and the biological digestion of proteins through enzymes. The small intestine can amount to 20 times the length of the cow, and most of the digestive process is completed here. The large intestine is the last segment of the tract through which undigested food passes. Its primary digestive activity is the absorption of water.

Questions 1–4

Label the diagram below.

*Choose **NO MORE THAN TWO WORDS** from the passage for each answer.*

The digestive tract of a cow

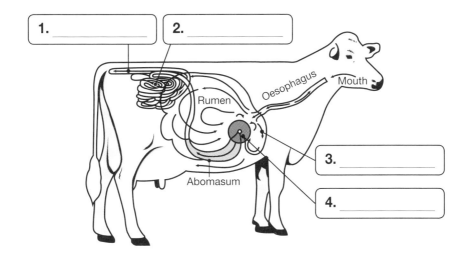

1. _____

2. _____

Oesophagus

Mouth

Rumen

Abomasum

3. _____

4. _____

Question Type 10　略図完成問題の攻略法

●**問題形式**　記述式の問題。空欄のある表や図式が与えられ、本文で説明されている内容と一致する部分の解答を記述する。

●**攻略法**　このタイプの設問では、本文を読み始める前に図面や表を見て、内容について推測することが有効でしょう。解答は本文の主旨ではなく、部分的な内容に関わるものが中心となります。記述式の問題なので、スペリングには注意しておきましょう。数字は英字でもアラビア数字でもどちらも可能です。「'（アポストロフィ）」での文字の省略は解答に含まれません。また、ハイフンで繋がった語は1語としてカウントされます。

●**実力強化のポイント**　本文の詳細を理解する語彙力、その内容と図表を関連づけて解答を見つけ出す読解力などが求められます。

例題の解答・解説

正解　**1** large intestine　**2** small intestine　**3** reticulum　**4** omasum

問題文全訳

6分間を目安にして、以下の問題文をもとに**設問1–4**に答えなさい。

牛の消化器官

❶牛の消化管は口、食道、4部位構成の胃、小腸と大腸から成り立っている。❷胃には第1胃、網胃、葉胃と第4胃がある。❸4つの部分のうち、第1胃が一番大きくて、更にいくつかの嚢に分かれている。❹第1胃の中の状態は微生物の繁殖に好ましく、ここで消化と発酵の過程が行われる。❺網胃は小袋に似たような作りで、体腔の前方に位置していて、飲み込んでしまった異物を取る役割がある。❻網胃は心臓に近いので、釘のように尖っている物を飲み込んでしまうと致命傷になりうる。❼葉胃は球体の形をしていて、第4胃への通路としての役割をはたし、消化物から水や他の物質を吸収する。❽第4胃は「真の胃」と呼ばれることもあり、その機能は塩酸による食べ物の化学分解と酵素によるタンパク質の生物学的消化である。❾小腸は牛の全長の約20倍もの長さになることがあり、消化過程の大部分がここで完了する。❿大腸は消化管の最後の部分で、不消化物がここを通る。⓫大腸で行われる主な消化活動は水分の吸収である。

設問1–4

以下の図を完成させよ。

それぞれの解答を本文から2語以内で選びなさい。

牛の消化管

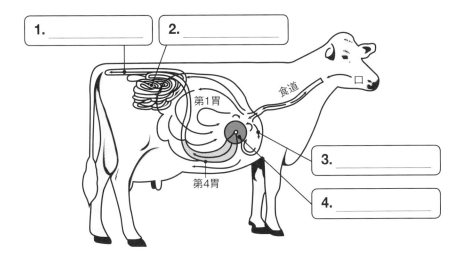

1. _____

2. _____

3. _____

4. _____

第1胃

食道

第4胃

第1章

設問TYPE

|解説|

1　（大腸）10文に消化管の最後の部分とある。

2　（小腸）9文に牛の全長の20倍の長さがあると述べられている。

3　（網胃）5-6文によると、心臓に近く葉胃の前の消化器官である。

4　（葉胃）7文に形状が球状とある。

⏱ **6 minutes**

*You should spend about 6 minutes on **Questions 1–3**, which is based on the reading passage below.*

Green Mathematicians

Scientists working at the John Innes Centre (JIC) in the county of Norfolk, England have theorised that plants have a mechanism resembling a chemical calculator that helps them to use energy reserves efficiently. During the day, when the sun is shining, plants perform photosynthesis, converting sunlight, water and carbon dioxide into starch. The plants then burn this stored starch to continue growing at night. 'If the starch store is used too fast, the plants will stop growing during the night. If the store is used too slowly, some of it will be wasted,' says study co-author Alison Smith.

As an experiment, biologists shut off the lights early on plants that had been accustomed to days and nights of equal length. Since the plants had not had enough time to store the usual amount of starch, they needed to recalculate the most efficient way to use their limited energy reserves, and they did so with no apparent difficulty. The researchers hypothesised that the plants receive information about the amount of starch and the time to dawn through two molecules. One of these molecules stimulates, or speeds up, starch degradation and the other molecule, which also acts as the plant's circadian clock, inhibits, or slows it down. It appears that a set of chemical reactions regulated by the relative numbers of these two molecules is responsible for controlling the rate of uptake of the starch.

Question 1–3

Answer the questions below.

*Choose **NO MORE THAN TWO WORDS** from the passage for each answer.*

1 What fuels the plants' growth after dark?

2 What was the ratio of day to night time the plants had before the experiment began?

3 What other function does the inhibitory molecule that slows starch degradation have?

Question Type 11　英問英答問題の攻略法

●**問題形式** 本文の内容について設問が複数あり、それぞれ指定された語数の英語で答える記述式の問題。解答の語は本文の中の表現を用いる。

●**攻略法** このタイプの設問では、本文の流れの順に設問が出されているので、自信のある質問の解答を見つけられると他の設問の解答を探しやすくなるでしょう。Type 10と同様に、スペリングには注意しておきましょう。数字は英字でもアラビア数字でもどちらも可能です。「'（アポストロフィ）」での文字の省略は解答に含まれません。また、ハイフンで繋がった語は1語としてカウントされます。

●**実力強化のポイント** 本文の特定の情報を正確に読み取る力、指示の内容に従って正解を見つける力が求められます。

例題の解答・解説

|正解| **1** starch　**2** equal (length)　**3** circadian clock

|問題文全訳|

6分間を目安にして、以下の問題文をもとに**設問1–3**に答えなさい。

緑色の数学者

1 ❶イギリスのノーフォーク郡にあるジョン・インズ・センターで研究をしている科学者たちは、植物はエネルギーの貯蓄を効率よく利用する助けとなる化学計算機に似通ったメカニズムを持つという理論を立てた。❷日中、日が照っている時は、植物は光合成を行ない、日光と水と二酸化炭素をデンプンに変える。❸植物はこの貯蓄されたデンプンを燃焼して、夜に成長を続ける。❹共同研究者のアリソン・スミスは「デンプンの貯蓄の使用が急すぎると、植物は夜間の成長を止めてしまう。❺貯蓄の使用がゆっくりすぎると、無駄になってしまうものもある」と言う。

2 ❶実験として、生物学者は昼夜の長さが同じであることに慣れている植物に対して、早めに明かりを消してみた。❷通常の量のデンプンを貯める十分な時間がなかったため、植物は限られた備蓄量のエネルギーを最も効率よく使う方法を計算し直さなければならなかったが、これといった問題なくやってのけてしまった。❸研究者は、植物がデンプンの量と夜明けまでの時間についての情報を2つの分子を通して受信しているという仮説を立てた。❹この分子の1つはデンプンの分解を刺激し早め、もう1つの分子

は植物の体内時計として機能し、デンプンの製造の分解を抑制し遅らせる。❺こうした2つの分子の相対的な数によって調節される一連の化学反応がデンプンの摂取率を制御しているようだ。

設問1-3

以下の設問に答えなさい。

それぞれの解答を2語以内で本文から選びなさい。

    1   日没後に植物の成長を促すものは何か。

    2   実験を始める前、植物にとっての昼と夜の時間の比率はどうだったか。

    3   デンプンの分解を抑制する分子が持つ他の機能は何か。

|解説|

1   1段落2-3文で、光合成により作られたデンプンは夜間に燃焼され植物の成長に使われると述べられている。

2   2段落1文に、実験では昼と夜が同じ長さであることに慣れている植物が光を浴びる時間を縮めるとある。

3   2段落4文で2種類の分子について言及があるが、デンプンの分解を遅らせる方の分子についてはcircadian clock（体内時計）として機能するとある。

第2章

リーディングセクション
問題演習

*You should spend about 20 minutes on **Questions 1–14**, which are based on the reading passage below.*

The Hidden Strengths of the Introvert

A   Many of us have taken personality quizzes in magazines or on the Internet, hoping that they will show us to be one type of person over another. Sometimes it is tempting to influence the result by modifying our answers. Wouldn't we all rather be courageous than cowardly, optimistic rather than pessimistic, relaxed rather than uptight? Many of us like to think of ourselves as extroverted rather than introverted. Extroverts are popular, fun-loving, and cool. Surely it's better to have lots of friends and go to parties than be a shy nerd? The notion that extroversion is superior is so ingrained in our culture that extroverted parents have even been known to send their children to psychiatrists in an attempt to 'cure' their child's quiet ways. And this happens despite the fact that introverts make up at least one-third of the population.

B   But what exactly is an introvert? An introvert is someone who prefers peace and quiet, and feels uncomfortable in high-stimulus environments. He or she tires quickly at parties, and needs to take frequent 'time-outs' in social situations. Signs of introversion appear at the earliest stage of life. Studies have shown that babies who react strongly to stimuli, such as hand-clapping, are more likely to grow up as introverts while those who react less are more likely to become extroverts. Many people believe introversion is about being shy or antisocial, but that's a misconception. Shyness derives from the fear that society will react negatively toward you. You can be introverted without having that fear at all. It is also possible to be a shy extrovert who performs well socially but experiences discomfort at the same time.

C   Western society seems obsessed with turning us into extroverts from the get-go. Picture the modern classroom. The days when kids sat at their desks and worked individually are long gone. Nowadays students sit facing each other as they work on countless group projects, even in subjects like math and creative writing. Kids who prefer to work by themselves don't fit in, and research shows that most teachers believe the ideal student is an extrovert—even though introverts tend to get higher grades. Colleges similarly focus on the extrovert. U.S. colleges, especially, grade you on your ability to speak out. At Harvard Business School, which often acts as a stepping stone to corporate success, the ability to take part in head-to-head, often gladiatorial, debates forms an integral part of the marking scheme. When they are not in the classroom, students are encouraged to take part in sports clubs or study groups that leave them little time to themselves.

D   This bias doesn't end when we leave school. The modern office is increasingly set up for maximum group interaction, and the open plan, with no walls and little privacy, has become the norm. We also structure our workplaces around extroverted behaviour such as brainstorming, even though studies show that people are more creative when working on their own rather than in a group environment, where the loudest voice often dominates the discussion. As Susan Cain puts it in her book *Quiet: The Power of Introverts in a World that Can't Stop Talking*, 'There's zero correlation between being the best talker and having the best ideas.'

E   So do we just have to accept that the extroverts will win all the spoils, leaving the introverts to slink away into a corner and deal with the situation as best they can? Luckily, the answer is 'No.' Despite the best efforts of the education system, a full 40% of executives describe themselves as introverts. While extroverts have the gift of the gab, the introverts' very lack of dominance can help them succeed within a certain type of business environment. Charismatic extroverts may be better at leading people who are prepared to accept the boss' word without question, but introverted leaders often

第2章

Exercise

produce better outcomes when their teams are proactive. In such setups, extroverted leaders might dominate discussions, preventing good ideas from coming to the fore.

F Introverted leaders are also better listeners, and tend to think before they speak. This tendency to be more careful with words is an asset in a position where it is costly to make mistakes. Introverted leaders like to dig deep, investigating issues and ideas thoroughly before moving on to new ones. They are drawn to meaningful conversations, not chit-chat, and they know how to ask great questions and really listen to the answers. Introverted leaders also prepare well, rehearsing speeches and delivering them in measured tones. Former President Obama is a good example of just such a leader. They also tend to be comfortable with the written word, which helps them better articulate their positions and document their actions. Finally, they embrace solitude, and these regular timeouts actually fuel their thinking, creativity and decision-making.

G So if you ever have the time to take a personality test and it indicates that you are an introvert, don't be dismayed. Don't say to yourself, 'I am shy and inhibited, and will never make it to the top.' Instead, you can reassure yourself that you are probably careful and reflective, and be proud that you share a personality trait with many of the great achievers, not just in the world of business, but across the spectrum of professions. Who wouldn't want to be in the company of distinguished individuals such as the writer J.K. Rowling, actor Harrison Ford, entrepreneur Bill Gates, and physicist Albert Einstein? Perhaps introversion carries the key to success, after all.

Questions 1–5

The Reading Passage has seven paragraphs **A–G**.

Which paragraph contains the following information?

*Write the correct letter **A–G** in boxes 1–5 on your answer sheet.*

NB *You may use any letter more than once.*

1   evidence of a bias against introversion at school
2   an example of an introverted leader who prepares speeches
3   how introversion can improve innovation at work
4   how introverts should feel upon taking a personality test
5   the differences between shyness and introversion

Questions 6–11

Do the following statements reflect the claims of the writer in the reading passage?

In boxes 6–11 on your answer sheet, write

> **YES**   *if the statement reflects the claims of the writer*
> **NO**   *if the statement contradicts the claims of the writer*
> **NOT GIVEN**   *if it is impossible to say what the writer thinks about this*

6   Introversion is a personality trait that many prefer not to have.
7   People who grow up to become introverts reacted less to stimuli as babies.
8   Those who are good at talking also tend to have the best ideas.
9   The open-plan office has become popular since the 1990s.
10   Wanting to be alone is a weak point for a leader.
11   Some of the most accomplished people have been introverts.

*Choose the correct letter **A, B, C** or **D**.*

Write your answers in boxes 12–14 on your answer sheet.

12 Some extroverts send their children to psychiatrists because they think

    A introversion is a disease caused by a defective gene.

    B their children's personality can be changed.

    C it is strange that parent and child should be so different.

    D their children are becoming too aggressive.

13 Leading business institutes expect students to

    A avoid sporting activities.

    B spend little time in study groups.

    C be good listeners as well as speakers.

    D debate each other aggressively.

14 Introverts should not be worried because

    A it is possible to be a successful introvert.

    B extroverts are promoted less often.

    C they are quicker to implement new ideas.

    D extroverts are easily dominated.

第2章

Exercise

NO TEST MATERIAL ON THIS PAGE

内向型の人の隠れた力

A ❶私たちの多くは、雑誌やインターネットで、あるタイプのうちのある人間だという判定が出ることを願いながら性格テストをやったことがある。❷時々、回答を変えて結果を変わるようにしたくなることもある。❸臆病より勇敢で、悲観的より楽観的で、神経質よりおおらかでいたいとみんな思うのではないだろうか。❹私たちの多くは自分を内向型ではなく外向型だと思いたがる。❺外向型人間は人気者で、面白いことが好きで、格好いい。❻確かに、内気なオタクでいるよりも友達が多くパーティーに出かけているほうが良い。❼外向性が良いという考えが文化に根付いているので、外向的な親は子供の大人しさを「治そう」として、精神科医のところに子供を連れていくことまで知られている。❽内向型人間が人口の少なくとも3分の1を占めているという事実にも関わらず、このようなことが起きる。

B ❶しかし内向型人間とは正確にはどのような人なのだろう。❷内向型人間は平穏と静けさを好み、刺激の強い環境にいると居心地が悪いと感じる人である。❸パーティーではすぐに疲れて、社交の場で頻繁に「タイム」をとる必要がある。❹内向性の兆候は人生の初期の段階で現れる。❺手をたたくような刺激に強く反応する赤ん坊は成長して内向型になる可能性が高く、一方でより反応の少ない赤ん坊は外向型になる可能性が高いと研究は示している。❻内向性とは内気で非社交的なことだと思っている人が多いが、それは誤解である。❼内気さは、社会が自分に対して否定的に反応するだろうという不安から生じる。❽全く不安がなくても内向型になりえる。❾社交上手だが同時に不安感を覚えるような、内気な外向型人間にもなりえるのだ。

C ❶西洋社会は最初から私達を外向型人間にする事にこだわっているようだ。❷現代の教室を思い描いてみればいい。❸子供達が机に座り個別に勉強していた時代はとうに消えた。❹最近は 数えきれないほど多くのグループ作業に取り組む時、数学や作文のような科目であっても、生徒達は互いに向き合って座る。❺一人で勉強することを好む子供はこれに適合せず、調査によると、内向型人間のほうがよい成績をとる傾向があっても、教師の大半は理想的な生徒は外向型なのだと考えている。❻大学も同様に外向型人間に焦点をあてている。特に米国の大学は堂々と発言する能力で成績をつける。❼ハーバード大学大学院経営学研究科は、企業で成功するた

めの足がかりの役目を果たすことが多いが、ここでは一対一のしばしば攻撃的な討論に参加する能力が成績評価の必須の部分となっている。❽教室外では、学生達はスポーツクラブや研究グループに参加することを奨励されるので、自分自身の時間はほとんどない。

D　❶学校を出てもこの偏見は終わらない。❷現在のオフィスはますます集団内のやり取りを最大限にするために設置されていて、壁が無く、プライバシーもほとんどない、仕切りのないオフィスが標準である。❸また、例えばブレインストーミングのような外向的な行動を中心として職場が構築されているので、グループの環境よりも一人で働くほうが創造的であると研究は示していても、議論を支配するのは声高な発言である。❹スーザン・ケインが著書『内向型人間の時代　社会を変える静かな人の力』の中で述べているように、「話し上手であることと最もアイディアが優れていることの間の相関関係はゼロだ」。

E　❶それでは、外向型人間が全ての特権を勝ち取り、内向型人間をこっそり隅に逃してできるだけその状況に対処させておくという事態を、私達は受け入れなければならないのだろうか。❷幸い、答えは「ノー」である。❸教育制度の最善の努力にもかかわらず、40％もの重役が自分を内向型だと述べている。❹話術の才能を持っているのは外向的な人だが、内向型人間の支配力不足こそがある種のビジネス環境で成功することに役立つことがある。❺カリスマ的な外向型人間は、疑いもなく上司の言葉を受け入れる人々を導くのが上手かもしれないが、チームが積極的に行動する時は、内向的な指導者の方が良い成果を生み出すことがよくある。❻そのような設定では、優れた考えが生まれるのを妨げ外向型の指導者は議論を支配しうる。

F　❶内向的な指導者は聞き上手でもあり、話す前に考える傾向がある。❷この言葉に注意深くなるという傾向は、誤りが損失となる状況においては強みである。❸内向的な指導者は深く掘り下げて、新しい物に移る前に問題や考えを徹底的に調査する。❹雑談ではなく意味のある会話に魅力を感じ、良い質問の仕方を心得ていて、答えをじっくり聞く。❺内向的な指導者は十分に準備も行い、スピーチを繰り返し練習し、慎重な口調で発表する。❻オバマ前大統領はまさにそのような指導者の良い例だ。❼彼らには活字を苦にしない傾向もあり、それは自分の立場を明確に述べて行動を立証することに役立つ。❽最後に、彼らは孤独を好み、こうした定期的な小休止が実際のところ思考、創造性、意思決定を促進する。

G　❶だから、もしあなたが性格テストを受けて内向型人間だという判定が出ても、がっかりすることはない。❷「自分は内気でためらいがちだから、成功は絶対にし

ない」と自分に言ってはいけない。❸それより、自分はおそらく注意深くて思慮深い人間なのだと自分にいいきかせて安心すればいい。そして、ビジネス界だけでなく多様な職業分野の偉人の多くと同じ人格的特徴を共有していることを誇りに思ってよい。❹作家J.K. ローリング、俳優ハリソン・フォード、起業家ビル・ゲイツ、物理学者アルベルト・アインシュタインの仲間になりたくない人がいるだろうか。❺結局のところ、おそらく内向性が成功の鍵を握っているのだ。

重要語句

☐ ingrained	〔形〕	染み付いた、根付いた
☐ from the get-go	〔副〕	始めから
☐ a stepping stone to success	〔名〕	成功への踏み石
☐ open plan	〔名〕	間仕切りのない空間
☐ As S puts it	〔熟〕	Sが言うように
☐ come to the fore	〔熟〕	水表面に現れる
☐ articulate …	〔動〕	…をはっきり述べる
☐ make it to the top	〔熟〕	頂点までたどりつく
☐ reassure …	〔動〕	…を安心させる

正解一覧

1 C	**2** F	**3** E	**4** G
5 B	**6** YES	**7** NO	**8** NO
9 NOT GIVEN	**10** NO	**11** YES	**12** B
13 D	**14** A		

問題文和訳

Questions 1–5

本文はA–Gの7段落である。以下の情報を含むのはどの段落か？
解答用紙の空欄1–5にA–Gを記入しなさい。
同じ文字を二度以上使用して良い。

1　学校での内向性に対する偏見の証拠
2　スピーチの準備をする内向的な指導者の例
3　どのようにして内向性が職場での革新を推し進めるか

4 性格テストを受ける際に内向型人間ならどのように感じるべきか

5 内気さと内向性の違い

1 正解 C

C段落全体で学齢時も大学でも学業で外向性が奨励される例を紹介している。

2 正解 F

F段落5〜6文にIntroverted leaders also prepare well, rehearsing speeches and delivering them in measured tones. Former President Obama is a good example of just such a leader.（内向的な指導者は十分に準備も行い、スピーチを繰り返し練習し、慎重な口調で発表する。オバマ前大統領はまさにそのような指導者の良い例だ）とある。

3 正解 E

E段落4〜5文で、内向的な指導者に著しい影響力が無いことで、意見が活発化して良い結果を生むとある。

4 正解 G

G段落3文に性格テストで内向型人間だと判定が出た場合でもyou can reassure yourself that you are probably careful and reflective（自分はおそらく注意深くて思慮深い人間なのだと自分にいいきかせて安心すればいい）とある。

5 正解 B

「内気さ」についてはB段落7〜8文でShyness derives from the fear that society will react negatively toward you. You can be introverted without having that fear at all.（内気さは、社会が自分に対して否定的に反応するだろうという不安から生じるが、全く不安がなくても内向型になりえる）とあり、「内向性」の説明は同じ段落の2文でAn introvert is someone who prefers peace and quiet, and feels uncomfortable in high-stimulus environments.（内向型人間は平穏と静けさを好み、刺激の強い環境にいると居心地が悪いと感じる人である。）と言及して筆者は区別している。

問題文和訳

Questions 6–11

以下の記述は本文の筆者の主張を反映しているか？

解答用紙の6–11の欄内に…を書きなさい。

YES	もし文が筆者の主張を反映しているなら
NO	もし文が筆者の主張に矛盾しているなら
NOT GIVEN	もし筆者が考えていることだと言うことができないなら

6 内向性は多くの人々が持っていたくない人格の特性である。

7 成長して内向性になる人々は、赤ん坊の時に刺激にあまり反応しなかった。

8 おしゃべりが得意な人々はまた優れた考えを持つ傾向がある。

9 間仕切りのないオフィスは1990年代以来人気になっている。

10 一人になりたいということは、指導者にとって弱点である。

11 達成者のなかには内向型の人もいる。

6 |正解| **YES**

A段落4文にMany of us also like to think of ourselves as extroverted rather than introverted.（私たちの多くは自分を内向型ではなく外向型だと思いたがる）とある。

7 |正解| **NO**

B段落5文にStudies have shown that babies who react strongly to stimuli, such as hand-clapping, are more likely to grow up as introverts while those who react less are more likely to become extroverts.（手をたたくような刺激に強く反応する赤ん坊は成長して内向型になる可能性が高く、一方でより反応の少ない赤ん坊は外向型になる可能性が高いと研究は示している）とあるので本文と逆の内容。

8 |正解| **NO**

D段落4文のThere's zero correlation between being the best talker and having the best ideas.（話し上手であることと最もアイディアが優れていることの間の相関関係はゼロだ）の主旨に反する。

9 |正解| **NOT GIVEN**

1990年代の記述はない。

10 |正解| **NO**

F段落8文にFinally, they embrace solitude, and these regular timeouts actually fuel their thinking, creativity and decision-making.（最後に、彼らは孤独を好み、こうした定期的な小休止が実際のところ思考、創造性、意思決定を促進する）とあるので弱点ではない。

11 |正解| **YES**

G段落で、内向型で成功した有名人の名前が列挙されている。

問題文和訳

Questions 12–14

正しいものをA, B, C, Dから選びなさい。

解答用紙の12–14の欄に解答を記入しなさい。

12 外向型の人のなかには、子供を精神科医に連れて行く者がいるのは、彼らが ▓▓▓▓▓ と考えるからだ。

 A 内向性は欠陥遺伝子が原因となる病気だ

 B 子供の人格は変えられる

 C 親と子供がとても異なるのは奇妙だ

 D 子供が暴力的になりすぎている

13 一流のビジネススクールは、学生達が ▓▓▓▓▓ ように期待する。

 A スポーツ活動を避ける

 B 研究グループではわずかな時間しか過ごさない

 C 話し上手でもあり聞き上手である

 D お互いに攻撃的に討論する

14 内向型は心配するべきではない。なぜなら

 A 成功する内向型になる可能性がある。

 B 外向型が昇進することの方が少ない。

 C より素早く新しいアイディアを実行に移す。

 D 外向型人間は簡単に圧倒できる。

12 |正解| B

A段落7文内のcure（治療する）は、人格を直すことを意味する。欠陥遺伝子や「子供が親と異なる」、「子供が暴力的」などの記述はない。

13 |正解| D

C段落7文に、head-to-head, often gladiatorial, debates（一対一のしばしば攻撃的な討論）に参加する能力が重視されるとある。

14 |正解| A

G段落第1文で、性格テストで内向型だという結果が出てもdon't be dismayed（がっかりすることはない）とある。また、第4文で内向型の著名人の名前が列挙されていて、最終文で内向型であることが成功の鍵であるかもしれないと結んでいる。

*You should spend about 20 minutes on **Questions 1–13**, which are based on the reading passage below.*

Cities of the Future

The mass migration of people from the countryside to the city that accompanied the economic shift from agriculture to manufacturing, technology, and services has now reached the point where just over half of the world's citizens are urban dwellers. Experts predict that by 2050 this figure will soar to 70%. An insatiable demand for housing has led to the creation of endless suburbs that are eating into the countryside around our cities. Suburban sprawl means that we often live long distances from the shops and workplaces that we travel to on a regular basis. This can result in an over-dependence on cars, with many of us making environmentally damaging daily journeys to and from scattered locations across our cities. City planners are watching this trend closely, and working tirelessly to solve these problems in their designs of cities of the future.

One possible solution is to develop smaller, high-density cities, known as 'compact cities', built around strategically placed green zones. Compact cities have the twin advantages of allowing people to live closer to their places of work, and losing less countryside to urban sprawl. Pedestrianisation is a key feature, which means that more journeys can be made on foot, leading to less air and noise pollution and a reduced carbon footprint. The OECD, citing the examples of Melbourne and Vancouver, has concluded that compact cities can protect the environment, promote regional growth, and offer a better quality of life than the more conventional, mostly unplanned cities.

Compact housing strategies can also benefit historical cities. It has been suggested that more compact housing in Paris could free up enough land to increase the city's green space by some 30%. As well as improving the 'lungs of the city', this action could preserve biodiversity and limit temperature rises in the case of a heat wave. For governments looking to save money, compact cities offer more efficient infrastructure investment and reduce the maintenance costs associated with transport, water supply, and waste disposal.

But the compact city isn't the only contender for future human habitation. Another kind of city that is tipped to thrive economically in the 21st century is the aerotropolis. Similar in form and function to a traditional metropolis built around a central city core with outlying suburbs, aerotropolises are designed around an airport on the principle that large, well-connected hubs contribute more to prosperity above all else. Industries that cluster in and around airports are often connected with time-sensitive manufacturing; e-commerce and logistics; hotels and exhibition centres, or offices for international businesspeople. As these businesses grow, the aerotropolis becomes a major urban destination where air travellers and locals alike can work, shop, and be entertained within walking distance of the airport.

According to John Kasarda, professor at the University of North Carolina and the best-known advocate for the concept of the aerotropolis, the number of passenger air journeys is expected to double over the next decade, and cities that can cater to the demand that this generates will have the ascendancy. Kasarda notes that airports are evolving as drivers of urban development in the 21st century just as seaports, railroads, and highways did before them.

Successful cities of this type need to be properly planned, with governing bodies comprising airport management, regional officials, and local business leaders leading the way. The development of New Songdo has been built entirely to serve Incheon Airport in South Korea, and Singapore Airport has been designed to be an integral part of the economically successful city it serves. Those who favour the aerotropolis see their shopping zones as evolving town squares, with outdoor cafes and other areas where people can sit and relax. Kasarda notes that Amsterdam's Schiphol Airport already has a museum that displays art exhibits, while Heathrow Airport hosts performances from the London Philharmonic Orchestra.

Yet despite the hype, as anyone who travels knows, airports are often soulless places that few people would visit by choice. The micromanaged zones of an airport are not, in reality, anything like a town square, but rather have all the character and spontaneity of a shopping mall. Nor are airport cities pure expressions of the market, as most 19th-century railway towns were, since the taxpayer is expected to make a major contribution to an environment created to serve the needs of business.

The shape of human habitation is constantly changing, and the world is big enough to accommodate many different configurations, but we should beware of abandoning the beauty and idiosyncrasy of our historical cities in the constant search for something new. An old cliché cautions us not to throw out the baby with the bathwater. As city planners rush to design the compact cities and aerotropolises of the future, let us hope that the cities rich in history and the rural villages with thatched cottages will not be completely abandoned.

Questions 1–6

Do the following statements agree with the information given in the reading passage?

In boxes 1–6 on your answer sheet, write

TRUE	*if the statement agrees with the information*
FALSE	*if the statement contradicts the information*
NOT GIVEN	*if there is no information on this*

1   Soon almost half the world's population will live in cities.
2   Melbourne is given as an example of an aerotropolis.
3   John Kasarda supports the concept of the aerotropolis.
4   New Incheon Airport was funded by the South Korean government.
5   Heathrow airport incorporates a town square.
6   Railroad towns grew up in response to market forces.

Questions 7–9

Complete the summary.

*Choose **NO MORE THAN TWO WORDS** from the passage for each answer.*

Write your answers in boxes 7–9 on your answer sheet.

The world's population is becoming urbanised, and planners are busy developing cities for the future. One possible model is the compact city. The high-density housing of this kind of development provides an antidote to the suburban **7** _____ that is spreading out into the countryside, while its environmentally friendly features reduce the residents' **8** _____. Another concept is the aerotropolis, an airport-based hub built on the principle that good connections are essential to prosperity. The aerotropolis currently attracts industries that need to be near an airport, and while they may be criticised for lacking character, it is hoped that over time they will become more like a **9** _____ with cultural as well as business attractions.

Questions 10–13

*Complete each sentence with the correct ending **A–F** below.*

*Write the correct letter **A–F** in boxes 10–13 on your answer sheet.*

10 Most cities today
11 Compact cities
12 Successful aerotropolises
13 Historical cities

    A need careful planning.
    B cope with a growing birth rate.
    C are convenient for visiting parks and forests.
    D suffer from environmental and other issues.
    E alleviate the effects of very hot days.
    F have valuable qualities we should not lose.

第2章

Exercise

NO TEST MATERIAL ON THIS PAGE

Exercise 02   解答解説

全文訳

未来都市

1 ❶地方から大都市圏への人間の大量流入は、農業から製造業、技術産業、サービス業への経済変化に伴い、現在、世界人口の半数以上が都会の住民であるという点まで達している。❷この数字は2050年までに70％に膨らむと専門家は予想している。❸飽くことのない住宅の需要は、都市周辺の田園地帯を浸食する際限なく拡がる郊外を生み出している。❹郊外のスプロール現象によって、私達が定期的に行く店や職場から遠いところに住むことになる。❺これは車を過度に依存する結果となり、私達の多くは都市に点在する場所の間での日々の移動で環境に害を及ぼしていることになる。❻都市計画者はこの傾向を注視して、未来都市の設計の中でこうした問題を解決しようと休みなく取り組んでいる。

2 ❶1つの可能な解決策は、計画的に配置された緑地帯を中心に建設される「コンパクトシティー」として知られる、小さめで高い密度の都市を開発することだ。❷コンパクトシティーには、職場の近くに住むことを可能にすることと周辺の田園地帯が都会のスプロール現象により失われることを抑えるという2つの利点がある。❸歩行者専用化が重要な特徴で、移動の大半は徒歩で行い、大気汚染、騒音公害を減らし、カーボンフットプリント（二酸化炭素排出量）の減少につながることを意味する。❹OECD*はメルボルンとバンクーバーの例を引用して、コンパクトシティーは環境を守り、地域の成長を促進し、従来のほとんど無計画な都市よりも、より良い生活の質を提供できると結論づけている。

3 ❶コンパクト住宅方式は歴史的な都市のメリットにもなる。❷パリにもっと多くのコンパクト住宅があれば、十分な広さの土地を確保して都市の緑地部分を約30％増やすことができるだろうと示唆されている。❸「都市の肺」を改善すると同時に、こうした活動は生物の多様性の保持と、熱波が発生した際の気温の上昇を制限することも可能になる。❹財源の節約を目指す政府にとって、コンパクトシティーはより効率の良いインフラの投資環境を提供し、輸送、水の供給、廃棄物処理に関わるメンテナンスのコストを削減する。

4 ❶しかし、コンパクトシティーだけが未来の人間の住まいの候補なのではない。❷21世紀に経済成長すると予想される他のタイプの都市は空港都市である。❸離れた場

80

所にある郊外を伴った中央都市部の周辺に築かれた昔ながらの主要都市と形態と機能は似ているが、大型で接続の良いハブ空港がとりわけ何よりも都市の繁栄に重要であるという原則に基づいて、空港都市は空港の周りに設計されている。❹空港内また周辺に密集する産業は、しばしば一刻を争うような業種と結びつく。例えば、電子商取引と物流、ホテルと展示センター、そして国際的なビジネスマンのオフィスなどである。❺これらのビジネスが成長するにつれて、空港都市は空港利用者も地元民も同様に空港の徒歩圏内で働き、買物して楽しむことができる主要な都会の目的地となる。

5 ❶ノースカロライナ大学の教授であり、空港都市の概念の提唱者として著名なジョン・キャサーダによれば、今後10年で空の旅の乗客数は2倍になると予想され、このことから生み出される需要をまかなえる都市が優勢になるだろう。❷港や鉄道や高速道路がかつてそうであったように、21世紀の都市開発の推進力として空港が進化しているとキャサーダは指摘している。

6 ❶このタイプで成功する都市は、空港経営者、地域の当局者、地元の企業リーダー達から成る管理体制が主導して適切に計画される必要がある。❷ソンド新都市の開発は完全に韓国の仁川国際空港の利便性を高めるように意図されたもので、シンガポール空港は経済的に成功した都市の必要にかなう不可欠な要素であるように設計されたものである。❸空港都市を支持する人々は、ショッピングゾーンは人々が座ってリラックスできる屋外のカフェや場所がある町の広場の進化形だと見なす。❹アムステルダムのスキポール空港はすでに美術品を展示する美術館を備え、ヒースロー空港ではロンドン・フィルハーモニー管弦楽団の公演を主催しているとキャサーダは指摘している。

7 ❶しかしながら、派手な宣伝にもかかわらず、旅をする人なら分かるように、空港は好んで訪れる人などほとんどいない、温かみのない場所である。❷実際、細部に渡り管理されている空港は町の広場とは似ても似つかず、そこにはむしろショッピングモールが持つ個性や衝動性がある。❸空港都市は、大概の19世紀の鉄道の町のように純粋に市場から表れたものでもない。なぜなら納税者は、ビジネスのニーズに応えるためにつくられた環境に大きく貢献をすることを期待されているからだ。

8 ❶人間の生活圏の形はたえず変化しており、この世界は様々な形態を受容するのに十分な広さがある。しかし、私達は新しさを求め続けて歴史的な都市の美しさや特異性を捨てることのないよう注意すべきだ。❷古い決まり文句にあるように、赤ん坊を風呂の水と一緒に捨てては行けない（大事な物を無用なものと一緒に捨ててはならない）。❸都市設計者達がこぞって未来のコンパクトシティーや空港都市を設計しても、歴史豊かな都市やわら葺き屋根の小屋のある田舎の村を完全に捨ててしまわないことを願いたい

ものだ。

*OECD：経済協力開発機構（Organisation for Economic Co-operation and Development の略称）

重要語句

☐ **insatiable**	〔形〕	とどまることを知らない、貪欲な
☐ **suburban sprawl**	〔名〕	郊外が拡がる現象
☐ **look to ...**	〔動〕	…に関心を向ける
☐ **thrive**	〔動〕	繁栄する ＝ prosper
☐ **hub**	〔名〕	商業、輸送の中心
☐ **advocate**	〔名〕	提唱者 ＝ proponent
☐ **governing bodies**	〔名〕	管理体制
☐ **comprise O**	〔動〕	O を構成する
☐ **hype**	〔名〕	誇大広告
☐ **configuration**	〔名〕	環境設定、外形、構成

正解一覧

1 FALSE	**2** FALSE	**3** TRUE
4 NOT GIVEN	**5** FALSE	**6** TRUE
7 sprawl	**8** carbon footprint	**9** town square
10 D	**11** E	**12** A
13 F		

問題文和訳

Questions 1–6

以下の文は本文中の情報と一致しているか？
解答用紙の空欄1–6の欄に次のように書きなさい。

TRUE	もし情報と一致すれば
FALSE	情報と矛盾すれば
NOT GIVEN	これに関する情報がなければ

1 まもなく世界人口のほぼ半数が都市で暮らすことになるだろう。

2　メルボルンは空港都市の例として挙げられている。

3　ジョン・キャサーダは空港都市の概念を支持している。

4　新仁川空港は韓国政府に資金提供を受けた。

5　ヒースロー空港は町の広場を内包している。

6　鉄道の町は市場の力に反応して成長した。

1　┃正解┃ FALSE

1段落1文に ... has now reached the point where just over half of the world's citizens are urban dwellers（…現在、世界人口の半数以上が都会の住民であるという点まで達している）とあるので未来形とSoonが誤り。

2　┃正解┃ FALSE

2段落4文目でメルボルンはコンパクトシティーの例として取り上げられているので誤り。

3　┃正解┃ TRUE

5段落1文でキャサーダはbest-known advocate for the concept aerotropolis（空港都市の概念の提唱者として著名）とある。

4　┃正解┃ NOT GIVEN

韓国政府が資金提供したという記述はない。

5　┃正解┃ FALSE

6段落に文化的催しの記述はあるが、町の広場が含まれているとの記述はなく、7段落2文で空港と町の広場が対比されている。

6　┃正解┃ TRUE

7段落3文のNor are airport cities pure expressions of the market, as most 19th-century railway towns were（空港都市は、大概の19世紀の鉄道の町のように純粋に市場から表れたものでもない）という文から鉄道の町は市場の影響が反映されてできた都市の例と読み取れるので正しい。

┃問題文和訳┃

Questions 7–9

要約を完成しなさい。

本文からそれぞれの解答を2語以内で選び、解答用紙の7–9の欄に記入しなさい。

世界中の人口が都会化して、都市計画者達は未来都市の開発に忙しい。可能性のあるモデルの1つがコンパクトシティーだ。この種の密度の高い住宅の開発は、田園地帯に拡がる郊外の **7** スプロール現象 に対する防衛手段を提供し、その一方で環境に優しい特徴が住民の **8** カーボンフットプリント（二

酸化炭素排出量）を削減する。もう一つの概念は空港都市で、優れた接続が都市の繁栄に不可欠であるという原理に基づく空港中心の拠点だ。空港都市は現在空港に近接する必要がある産業を誘致しているが、特徴の無いことが批判される一方で、時間をかけて文化的にも、商業的にも魅力ある **9** 町の広場 の雰囲気を持つようになることが望まれる。

---

7 |正解| **sprawl**
コンパクトシティーの利点は2段落2文に losing less countryside to urban sprawl（周辺の田園地帯が都会のスプロール現象により失われることを抑える）とあり、郊外のスプロール現象を防ぐことにつながる。

8 |正解| **carbon footprint**
2段落3文にさらなる利点として環境を守ることが言及されている。

9 |正解| **town square**
6段落3文から進化する町の広場の言及があり、7、8段落で新しさをもとめることは特異性を失い、shopping mall と変わらないと述べている。これに対して town square は人々がリラックスできる望ましい場所である。

問題文和訳

Questions 10–13
それぞれの文を以下の正しい結末A–Fと結んで完成しなさい。
解答用紙の10–13の欄にA–Fを記入しなさい。

10 今日のほとんどの都市は
11 コンパクトシティーは
12 成功する空港都市は
13 歴史的都市は

  A 注意深く計画する必要がある。
  B 増加する出生率に対処する。
  C 公園や森を訪れるのに都合がよい。
  D 環境その他の問題に苦しむ。
  E 非常に暑い日の影響を軽減する。
  F 私達が失うべきではない価値ある特徴を備えている。

10 |正解| **D**
1段落5文に環境問題、遠距離の職住についての言及がある。

11 |正解| E

3段落3文に熱波の場合に気温の上昇を制限する記述がある。

12 |正解| A

6段落1文で適切に計画される必要があると述べられている。

13 |正解| F

8段落3文に歴史豊かな都市の特徴が捨てられてしまわないことを望むとある。

第2章 ■ 解答解説

time: 20 minutes

*You should spend about 20 minutes on **Questions 1–13**, which are based on the reading passage below.*

Questions 1–5

*The reading passage has nine paragraphs, **A–I**.*

*Choose the correct heading for paragraphs **B** and **E–H** from the list of headings below.*

*Write the correct number, **i–ix**, in boxes 1–5 on your answer sheet.*

	List of Headings
i	The three laws of motion
ii	Other activities
iii	Newton's early life
iv	Investigative method
v	Focusing on optics
vi	Newton's sensitivity
vii	In his own words
viii	Publishing a great work
ix	New theories and working in isolation

Example	Paragraph **A**	*Answer*	**iii**
1	Paragraph **B**		
Example	Paragraph **C**	*Answer*	**v**
Example	Paragraph **D**	*Answer*	**viii**
2	Paragraph **E**		
3	Paragraph **F**		
4	Paragraph **G**		
5	Paragraph **H**		
Example	Paragraph **I**	*Answer*	**vii**

The Life of Isaac Newton

A　Isaac Newton (1642–1727) was born on Christmas Day, 1642, in the county of Lincolnshire. His father, a prosperous farmer, had died three months earlier. When Newton was three, his mother remarried and went to live with her new husband, the Reverend Barnabus Smith, leaving her son in the care of his maternal grandmother. From the age of 12 Newton studied at the King's School in Grantham, but when he was 17 his mother, then widowed for the second time, took him out of school and put him to work managing a farm. He had little talent for farming, and hated it. Luckily for Newton and the world, a master at his old school persuaded his mother to send her son back to school so that he might complete his education.

B　In June 1661, he was admitted to Trinity College, Cambridge. At that time, the college's teachings were based on the ideas of Aristotle, which Newton absorbed alongside those of the modern philosopher Descartes and astronomers Copernicus, Galileo, and Kepler. In 1665, Newton began to develop a mathematical theory that later became known as calculus. Soon after he obtained his degree in August 1665, the university temporarily closed as a precaution against the Great Plague. Newton returned to his mother's house, and he later described the two years he spent in isolation there as the most productive of his life. During this time, he developed his theories on calculus, optics, and the law of gravitation, although he began to show the reticence that was to become a hallmark of his life by not publishing his works until many years later. In 1667, he returned to Cambridge as a fellow of Trinity College.

C　In 1669, Newton was appointed Lucasian Professor of Mathematics, and from 1670 to 1672 he lectured on optics. During this period, he investigated the refraction of light. He demonstrated that it was possible to split white light into a spectrum of colours by shining it through a prism, and that a second prism could recompose the multicoloured spectrum into white light. He also separated out a coloured beam and shone it on various objects to show that the coloured light does not change its properties, but stays the same colour. He used this knowledge to build the first known reflecting telescope, which he introduced to the Royal Society in 1671.

D　Newton suffered a nervous breakdown in 1675, and took several years to recover. In 1679, he returned to his work on gravitation and its effect on the orbits of planets, and his research received a stimulus when a comet appeared in the winter of 1680–1681. He worked out that the movement of planetary orbits would follow an elliptical form, and devoted the period from late 1684 to early 1686 to proving this idea. In 1687, he combined the fruits of his research to publish one of the most influential works on physics of all time. He called it *Philosophiae Naturalis Principia Mathematica* (*Mathematical Principles of Natural Philosophy*), often shortened to the '*Principia*'.

E　In a time when scientific investigation was largely hit-and-miss, Newton invented a universal scientific method, which he presented in the *Principia* as a set of four rules for scientific reasoning. By their application, Newton formulated the universal laws of nature with which he was able to unravel virtually all of the unsolved problems of his day. However, Newton went much further than outlining his rules for reasoning by actually describing how they might be applied to the solution of a given problem. The analytic method he invented exceeded the more philosophical and less scientifically rigorous approaches of Aristotle, and refined Galileo's experimental methods.

F　In the *Principia*, Newton also formulated the three laws of motion that enabled many of the advances of the Industrial Revolution which was soon to follow. In modern form, the first law (also known as the law of inertia) states that an object at rest tends to stay at rest, and that a moving object tends to continue moving

第
2
章

Exercise

unless acted upon by an external force. The second law states that acceleration is produced when a force acts on a mass. The greater the mass, the greater the force needed to accelerate the object. The third law states that for every action there is an equal and opposite reaction. A common example is two ice skaters pushing against each other and moving apart in opposite directions. Newton also defined the law of universal gravitation, using the Latin word *gravitas* (weight) for the effect that would later become known as gravity. Newton himself often told the story that he was inspired to formulate his theory of gravitation by watching an apple fall from a tree. This account is thought to be true, although no one now believes that the apple actually hit him on the head.

G   Newton's efforts did not go solely into scientific discovery. He also served as member of Parliament for Cambridge University from 1689–90 and 1701–2, although by all accounts his only comments were to complain about a draught in the chamber and ask that the window be closed. He was much more active in his role in the Royal Mint, the organisation responsible for England's coinage. He took an official post in this institution in 1696, and became Master of the Mint some years later. At this time in England's history, counterfeiting was rife—Newton estimated that about 20 percent of all coins were fake—but identifying and catching wrongdoers was a difficult task. Newton managed to gather the necessary evidence by disguising himself and frequenting bars and similar drinking establishments. He had himself made a justice of the peace (a judge) in all the counties around London, and successfully prosecuted 28 counterfeit coiners.

H   Despite his undisputed brilliance, Newton was extremely sensitive to criticism. When Robert Hooke, a fellow member of the Royal Society, criticised some of Newton's ideas, Newton was so offended that he gave up public debate, and the two men remained on poor terms until Hooke's death. Newton also had a long-running dispute with Leibniz. Newton falsely accused Leibniz of plagiarism over the discovery of calculus, which both men had, in fact, discovered of their own accord. Psychiatrist Simon Baron-Cohen believes that Newton suffered from what is now referred to as Asperger's syndrome.

I   While Newton was not known for his modesty, he made two statements that reveal a humble perspective about his place in the world. While accepting that his work was groundbreaking, he also acknowledged his debts to Kepler and Galileo, saying, 'If I have seen further it is by standing on the shoulders of giants.' In a later memoir, Newton wrote: 'I do not know what I may appear to the world, but to myself I seem to have been only like a boy playing on the sea-shore, and diverting myself in now and then finding a smoother pebble or a prettier shell than ordinary, whilst the great ocean of truth lay all undiscovered before me.'

Questions 6–9

Look at the following statements and the list of dates of events in Isaac Newton's life.
Match each statement with the date it relates to.
Write the correct letter A–F in boxes 6–9 on your answer sheet.

6   He begins to suffer from a mental disorder.
7   He ceases to be a Member of Parliament.
8   He commences his university education.
9   A comet appears in the sky.

	Dates of Events in Isaac Newton's Life
A	1642
B	1661
C	1672
D	1675
E	1680
F	1702

Questions 10–13

Complete the summary below.

Choose **ONE WORD ONLY** *from the passage for each answer.*

Write your answers in boxes 10–13 on your answer sheet.

Isaac Newton's Achievements

While Sir Isaac Newton is best known for his theory of gravity, which posits that objects attract each other across a distance, he also contributed a great deal to the field of optics. While investigating the refraction of light he made two important observations: white light shone through a prism would split into different colours; and, it was possible to **10** _____ the spectrum of colours back into white light by using a second prism. This knowledge was subsequently used to construct the first reflecting **11** _____. Newton is also known for the three laws of motion. The first law states that an object at rest will remain at rest, and that one in motion stays in motion unless an external force acts upon it. The second law states that acceleration is produced when a force acts on a mass. The third law states that for every action there is an equal and opposite reaction. Finally, Newton is credited with developing calculus. The fact that Leibniz was also recognised for its development led to a long **12** _____. Newton refused to accept that Leibniz was innocent and ended up accusing him of **13** _____.

Exercise 03 解答解説

全文訳

アイザック・ニュートンの人生

A ❶アイザック・ニュートン（1642–1727）は1642年のクリスマスの日にリンカンシャー州で生まれた。❷父は成功した農夫で3カ月前に亡くなっていた。❸ニュートンが3歳の時、母親は再婚して新たな夫のバーナバス・スミス牧師と暮らすようになり、息子を母方の祖母に預けた。❹12歳からニュートンはグランサムのキングズスクールで学んだが17歳の時、母親はまた未亡人になり、学校をやめさせて彼を農場経営の仕事に就けた。❺彼には農業の才能がほとんどなく仕事を嫌がった。❻ニュートンにも世界にとっても幸いなことに、彼の元の学校の校長が母親を説得して学業を修了できるように復学させた。

B ❶1661年6月、彼はケンブリッジ大学トリニティーカレッジに入学した。❷当時、大学の授業はアリストテレスの思想に基づいていたが、ニュートンは近代哲学者デカルト、天文学者コペルニクス、ガリレオ、ケプラーの思想も吸収した。❸1665年、後に微積分として知られるようになる数学的理論を構築し始めた。❹1665年8月、学位取得後間もなく、大流行のペストに対する予防策として大学が一時的に閉鎖された。❺ニュートンは母親の家に戻った。そこで孤独に過ごした2年間を、人生で最も生産的な時期であったと後に述べている。❻彼の人生の特徴となる寡黙な姿勢を示し始めて、何年も後になるまで研究を発表することはなかったが、この間に、微積分、光学、万有引力の法則を発展させた。❼1667年、トリニティーカレッジのフェロー職としてケンブリッジ大学に戻った。

C ❶1669年、ニュートンはルーカス教授職*に任命されて、1670年から1672年まで光学について講義した。❷この間、彼は光の屈折を研究した。❸プリズムを通して白色光をスペクトル（虹状の色帯）に分光させ、さらに2つ目のプリズムでその混合色のスペクトルを白色光に再構成することが可能だと証明した。❹また、色のついた光線を分光させて様々な物体を照らしても、色のついた光線はその特性を変えることなく同じ色のままであることを示した。❺この知識を利用して、知られている中で最初の反射望遠鏡を作成し、1671年に王立協会に披露した。

D ❶ニュートンは1675年、神経衰弱に苦しみ回復に数年を要した。❷1679年、引力そして惑星の軌道に対する引力の影響の研究に戻り、1680年から1681年にかけて

の冬の彗星の出現に研究上刺激を受けた。❸惑星の軌道の動きは楕円形になることに気づき、1684年後半から1686年の初めまでの期間をその証明に充てた。❹1687年その成果をまとめて、時代を超えて物理学に最も大きな影響がある研究の1つを発表した。❺彼は「自然哲学の数学的原理」と題したが、しばしば「プリンキピア」と略される。

E　❶科学の研究が主に運任せだった時代に、ニュートンは普遍的な科学的手法を考えだし、「プリンキピア」の中で、科学的推論法の4つのルールとして発表した。❷その応用により、当時解決できなかったほぼすべての問題を解くことが出来る普遍的な自然法を公式化した。❸しかし、ニュートンは特定の問題解決に応用する方法を実際に説明することによって推論のルールを概説する以上のことをした。❹彼が編み出した分析的方法は、アリストテレスの哲学的だが科学的に厳密さが欠けている方法をしのぎ、ガリレオの実験方法より洗練されていた。

F　❶「プリンキピア」の中で、ニュートンは間もなく訪れる産業革命の進歩の多くを可能にする3つの運動の法則も公式化した。❷近代の形式で、第1の法則（慣性の法則としても知られる）は、外的な力が働かないかぎり、休止している物体は休止したままの傾向があり、動く物体は動き続ける傾向があると述べる。❸第2の法則は、力が物体に働くと、加速が生じると述べる。❹物体が大きいほど、物体の加速に必要な力がますます大きくなる。❺第3の法則は、すべての動きに対して等しい反対の反応があると述べる。❻一般的な例は、2人のアイススケーターが互いに押し合うと、逆方向に離れ離れになる。❼また、ニュートンは万有引力の法則を定義し、ラテン語のgravitas（重さ）という言葉を使って、後に引力として知られるようになるその効果を表した。❽リンゴが木から落ちるのを見て、引力の理論が思い浮かんだのだと彼自身はよく話していた。❾この話は本当だと考えられているが、そのリンゴが実際彼の頭を直撃したなどと信じる者はだれもいない。

G　❶ニュートンの奮闘は科学的発見だけではなかった。❷1689–90年と1701–02年にケンブリッジ大学を代表する議員もしたが、誰に聞いても、彼の発言は会議所のすきま風の不平を言って、窓を閉めるように頼んだ一言だけだった。❸それよりも王立造幣局、イングランドの貨幣の鋳造に責任を負う組織の役職で活動的だった。❹1696年この組織の正式な職員になり、数年後には王立造幣局長になった。❺英国の歴史上、この時代はニセ金造りが横行し、ニュートンは約20%の硬貨が偽物だと推定したが、犯人を特定し捕らえるのは難しい任務だった。❻ニュートンは変装をして頻繁にバーなどの酒場に出入りし、なんとか自分で必要な証拠集めをした。❼彼はロンドン周辺のすべての州の治安判事（裁判官）に任命してもらい、28

人のニセ金造りを告訴するのに成功した。

H ❶明らかに素晴らしい才能を持っていたにもかかわらず、ニュートンは批評に過敏だった。❷王立協会の会員だったロバート・フックが、あるニュートンの考えを批判した際に公の討論を途中で打ち切るほど立腹し、フックが死ぬまで気まずい間柄のままだった。❸また、ライプニッツとも長期に渡る論争をした。❹微積分の発見に関するライプニッツの盗用を訴えたが、これはニュートンの誤りであり、実際両者とも自発的に発見していた。❺精神科医サイモン・バロン‐コーエンは、ニュートンが現在アスペルガー症候群と呼ばれている障害を患っていたのだと考えている。

I ❶ニュートンの謙遜ぶりは知られていなかったが、世の中での自分の立場に対する彼の謙虚な視点を表す2つの言葉がある。❷自分の研究は画期的だったと認めながらも、ケプラーとガリレオのおかげであることを認めて「私が（他の人々よりも）遠くを見ることができていたのだとすれば、それは巨人たちの肩に乗っていたからです。」と言った。❸後の回想録に「私が世の中でどう見られているかわからないが、自分は、浜辺で遊び、時々ふつうよりつるつるの小石やかわいい貝を見つけて楽しむ少年にすぎず、真実の大海は、目の前にすべて覆い隠されたままで横たわっていたのだ。」と書いた。

*ルーカス教授職：ケンブリッジ大学の数学関連分野の教授職の1つ。名誉ある地位であり、2009年まではスティーブ・ホーキング博士もこの地位にあった。

重要語句

☐ **master**	〔名〕校長《headmaster とも。米語では principal》	
☐ **in isolation**	〔副〕孤立して	
☐ **reticence**	〔名〕寡黙、遠慮	
☐ **devote O to ...ing**	〔熟〕O を…することに充てる	
☐ **formulate ...**	〔動〕（法律、計画、政策など）…をまとめる、…を公式化する	
☐ **inertia**	〔名〕慣性	
☐ **rife**	〔形〕（病気、飢餓、問題などが）流行して	
☐ **justice of the peace**	〔名〕治安判事	
☐ **on ... terms**	〔熟〕…の間柄で	
☐ **sense of perspective**	〔名〕物事を冷静に見る目	
☐ **divert oneself in ...**	〔動〕…で楽しむ	

正解一覧

1 ix	**2** iv	**3** i	**4** ii
5 vi	**6** D	**7** F	**8** B
9 E	**10** recompose	**11** telescope	**12** dispute
13 plagiarism			

問題文和訳

Questions 1–5

本文はA–Iの9段落である。下の見出しリストから段落Bと段落E–Hの正しい見出しを選び、解答用紙1–5の欄にi–ixを記入しなさい。

```
           見出しのリスト
 i    運動の3法則
 ii   他の活動
 iii  ニュートンの初期の人生
 iv   研究方法
 v    光学に焦点をあてる
 vi   ニュートンの過敏さ
 vii  彼自身の言葉で
 viii 素晴らしい研究を発表
 ix   新たな理論と孤独な中での研究
```

例	**A** 段落	解答	iii
1	**B** 段落		
例	**C** 段落	解答	v
例	**D** 段落	解答	viii
2	**E** 段落		
3	**F** 段落		
4	**G** 段落		
5	**H** 段落		
例	**I** 段落	解答	vii

1 |正解| ix

B段落に大学が閉鎖された2年間に一人で研究して過ごしたという記述がある。

2 |正解| iv

E段落でニュートンがuniversal scientific method（普遍的な科学的手法）とanalytic method（分析的方法）を考え出したとある。

3 |正解| i

F段落1文にthree laws of motion（3つの運動の法則）とあり、この法則についての説明が続いてる。

4 |正解| ii

G段落では議員や造幣局長としての活動が言及されている。

5 |正解| vi

H段落冒頭の表現sensitive to criticism（批判に敏感）という表現から内容が判断できる。

問題文和訳

Questions 6–9

以下の記述とアイザック・ニュートンの人生の出来事についての年号リストを見なさい。

関連するものを結び、解答用紙6–9の欄にA–Fの正しいものを記入しなさい。

6 精神障害に苦しみ始める。

7 議員であるのを辞める。

8 大学教育を開始する。

9 空に彗星が現れる。

アイザック・ニュートンの人生の出来事についての年号
A 1642年
B 1661年
C 1672年
D 1675年
E 1680年
F 1702年

6　|正解|　D

D段落1文目にnervous breakdown（神経衰弱）に苦しんだとある。

7　|正解|　F

G段落2文目に1689–90年と1701–02年に議員をしたとあるので、1702年は辞めた年となる。

8　|正解|　B

B段落冒頭に大学入学の言及がある。

9　|正解|　E

D段落2文目に1680–81年に彗星が出現したことが記述されている。

問題文和訳

Questions 10–13

以下の要約を完成させなさい。

それぞれの解答を本文から1語で選びなさい。

解答用紙の解答欄10–13に解答を記入しなさい。

アイザック・ニュートンの業績

アイザック・ニュートン卿は、物体がある距離間で互いに引きよせるのだとする引力の理論で最も良く知られているが、彼はまた光学の分野でも大きな貢献をした。光の屈折の研究で2つの重要な観察をした。まず、白色光がプリズムを通して異なる色に分光すること、そして、第2のプリズムを使うことによって様々な色のスペクトルを白色光に **10** 再構成することができた。この知識は後に最初の反射 **11** 望遠鏡を製作するのに使われた。また、ニュートンは3つの運動法則で有名である。第1の法則は外的な力が作用しない限り、静止している物体は静止したままであり、運動している物体は運動し続ける。第2の法則では、加速度は物体に力が働く時に生じる。第3の法則は、どの力にも作用と反作用があるというものだ。最後に、ニュートンは微積分学を展開させた功績がある。ライプニッツもその発展をみとめられていたという事実により、長い **12** 論争が起こった。ニュートンはライプニッツが無実だと認めることを拒否し、最終的に自分の研究を彼が **13** 盗作したと訴えるに至った。

10　|正解|　recompose

second prismという語句に注目して、C段落3文から文脈に合う単語を選択する。

11 |正解| telescope

2つの副詞subsequently「のちに」とfirst「最初の」に注目してプリズムの実験の後に初めて作られたものは何か考えてＣ段落5文から単語を選択する。

12 |正解| dispute

形容詞longで修飾されていることに注目する。ライプニッツとの関係において長かったものはＨ段落3文に言及がある。

13 |正解| plagiarism

accuse A of Bで「Bの理由にAを非難する」の意味だが、ニュートンが盗作を理由にライプニッツを非難したことがＨ段落4文で説明されている。

第2章

解答解説

03

*You should spend about 20 minutes on **Questions 1–13,** which are based on the reading passage below.*

The Gaia Theory

The Gaia Theory hypothesises that the components of planet Earth have evolved together to create a self-regulating system. The mechanisms which maintains the equilibrium of the earth's global temperature, atmospheric content, and ocean salinity are analogous to those of a human body which requires equilibrium of blood flow and oxygen content. Seen in this way, the earth resembles a living organism that sustains the conditions suitable for its own survival. As an example, even though the sun shines about 30 percent more brightly than it did when life began almost four billion years ago, the earth has reacted to maintain temperatures at levels suitable for life.

The Gaia theory was developed in the late 1960s by British scientist and inventor Dr James Lovelock, who named it after an ancient Greek goddess that personified the earth, and in the time since the theory was first formulated, many of the mechanisms by which Earth regulates itself have been identified. Cloud formation is an excellent example of this process. Previously, it was thought that cloud formation over the ocean was solely a chemical phenomenon, but it has now been found to be a function of the metabolism of oceanic algae, which produce sulphur molecules (as a waste gas) that form the condensation nuclei for raindrops. These cloud formations help to regulate Earth's temperature while also returning sulphur to terrestrial ecosystems, and so plays a vital part in sustaining life. Taking a similar example of the air we breathe, Lovelock captures the essence of the system thus: 'The air is to life just as is the fur to a cat or the nest for a bird… For life on Earth, the air is our protection against the cold depths and fierce radiation of space.'

This feedback system can be illustrated by the workings of Daisyworld, an imaginary planet the same size as the earth, orbiting a sun just like ours. In the beginning, Daisyworld is entirely covered with black and white daisies. The black daisies have darker petals, which are better at absorbing light for photosynthesis than the white daisies. The white daisies' petals are better at reflecting light than those of the black daisies, so the white daisies can avoid overheating. At first, Daisyworld has equal numbers of black and white daisies, but as the black daisies are more efficient at absorbing light, they gain the advantage, and proliferate. They begin to outnumber the white daisies, and soon there are so many of them that they are heating up the entire planet. As the temperature rises, the black daisies begin to die off, but the white daisies tend to survive because they are better at reflecting the sun's light. Soon, the white daisies have spread throughout Daisyworld. But now that the planet is covered with white daisies, so much heat from the sun is reflected away that the temperature begins to drop. The black daisies are then able to take advantage of the cold temperatures due to their superior photosynthesis efficiency. More black daisies appear, which heats up the planet once more. The cycle continues, with black daisies and white daisies proliferating and dying off in turn.

The evidence gathered in support of the Gaia theory is now considerable, but its usefulness also lies in how it forces us to look at the earth from an unfamiliar perspective and address fundamental questions about its nature. All of the earth's creatures, from bacteria to whales, are potentially important to its well-being. We must take seriously the death of any creature, whether a great whale or a tiny virus, because they all play their part. When we eliminate one of these from Earth, we have destroyed a part of ourselves, for we also are a part of Gaia. As the Elizabethan poet John Donne put it, 'And therefore never send to know for whom the bell tolls; It tolls for thee.'

The chief fear among Gaia supporters is that the ability of Earth to self-regulate in our favour may be reaching its limits as human beings put the planet under an unsustainable stress. Since the industrial revolution, the warming effect that arose as a by-product of human activities has raised temperatures higher than at any other time since the end of the last ice age, with the biggest upward trend occurring in the last century. If carbon dioxide emissions continue to grow, then by 2100 global temperatures will reach levels never before seen by homo sapiens. Gaia will have to respond by creating a new equilibrium. We can only hope that this equilibrium will be one that is also compatible with sustaining human life.

Complete the summary.
Choose **ONE WORD ONLY** from the passage for each answer.
Write your answers in boxes 1–4 on your answer sheet.

According to the Gaia theory, our planet functions in a way comparable to a
1 _____ living organism. In many ways, the earth resembles a human
2 _____ maintaining the conditions necessary for survival. Naming the
theory after a **3** _____ who symbolised the earth, Dr Lovelock created a
rich image of the ecosystem: the **4** _____ is to the earth what the fur is to
a cat.

Questions 5 and 6

Choose **TWO** letters, **A–E**.
Write your answers in boxes 5 and 6 on your answer sheet.
NB Your answers may be given in either order.

Which **TWO** of the following factors influencing the process of cloud
formation are mentioned in the text?

> **A** chemical processes of algae
> **B** phosphorus molecules
> **C** ocean tides
> **D** animal metabolism
> **E** surplus gas

Questions 7–10

Complete the sentences below.

Choose ONE WORD ONLY from the passage for each answer.

Write your answers in boxes 7–10 on your answer sheet.

7   Black daisies' petals are better at _____ the sunlight than those of white daisies.

8   White daisies are more efficient at _____ the sun's rays.

9   The ability to use _____ with greater efficiency allows black daisies to proliferate in colder climates.

10   As black daisies _____ white daisies, the temperature of Daisyworld rises.

Questions 11–13

Do the following statements agree with the information given in the reading passage?

In boxes 11–13 on your answer sheet, write

TRUE	*if the statement agrees with the information*
FALSE	*if the statement contradicts the information*
NOT GIVEN	*if there is no information on this*

11   The Gaia theory was developed in the early 1960s by James Lovelock.

12   Daisies can be categorised into two basic types on the earth.

13   We should take seriously the death of any organism.

ガイア理論

1 ❶ガイア理論は、地球の複数の構成要素が自己調節システムを作るために共に進化してきたのだと仮定している。❷地球全体の気温、大気に含まれる要素、海洋の塩分濃度の均衡状態を維持するメカニズムは、身体が血流や酸素含有量の均衡を維持するメカニズムに似ている。❸このように考えると、地球は自らの生存に適した状態を持続する生物に似ている。❹例として、太陽はほぼ40億年前に生命が始まった時より約30%明るく輝いているが、地球は生物に適したレベルの気温を維持するために反応してきた。

2 ❶ガイア理論は、1960年代後半に英国の科学者であり発明家でもあるジェームズ・ラブロック博士によって構築されたもので、彼は地球を擬人化した古代ギリシャの女神にちなんで名前をつけた。この理論が最初に体系化されて以来、地球が自己調節しているメカニズムの多くが確認されてきた。❷雲の形成はこのプロセスの優れた例だ。❸以前は大洋上の雲の形成は単に化学的な現象だと考えられていたが、今は大洋の藻類の代謝機能であると突き止められており、藻類は雨粒の凝縮核を作る硫黄分子を(排ガスとして)作り出す。❹こうした雲の形成は地球の気温を調節するのに役立ち、その間硫黄を再び地球の生態系に還元し、生物の維持に重要な役割を果たしている。❺私達が呼吸する空気についての同様の例をあげながら、ラブロックはそのシステムの要素を次のようにとらえている。「空気と生物の関係はまさに毛皮とネコ、または鳥にとっての巣の関係と同じだ。地球上の生物にとって、空気は厳しい寒さや猛烈な宇宙の放射線から保護するものである。」

3 ❶この帰還方式は地球と同じ大きさで、私達と丁度同じように太陽の軌道をまわる、想像上の惑星デイジーワールド*の構造で例証できる。❷最初、デイジーワールドは完全に黒と白のデイジーにおおわれている。❸黒のデイジーは黒い花びらを持ち、白いデイジーより光合成のために光をよく吸収する。❹白いデイジーの花びらは黒いデイジーの花びらよりよく光を反射するので、白いデイジーは地球の加温を回避できる。❺初め、デイジーワールドには同数の黒と白のデイジーがあるのだが、黒いデイジーはより効率的に光を吸収するので優勢になり、繁茂する。❻白いデイジーの数を上まわり、ほどなくあまりにも数が多くなるため、惑星全体の温度を引き上げる。❼温度が上昇するにつれ、黒いデイジーは枯れ始めるが、白いデイジーは太陽の光を反射するのに優れているのでよく生き残る。❽そのうちに、白いデイジーがデイジーワールド中に拡が

る。❾しかし、今では惑星が白いデイジーで覆われているので、太陽からの熱の大部分は反射されて気温が下がり始める。❿そうなれば、黒いデイジーは光合成の効率性が優れているので、寒い気温を優位に利用することができる。⓫より多くの黒いデイジーが現れ、もう一度惑星の気温が上がる。⓬黒いデイジーと白いデイジーが交互に繁茂しては枯れるという周期が続く。

4 ❶ガイア理論を支持して集められた論拠は今や相当数あるが、理論としての有用性は、未知の視点から地球を見て、その本質についての根本的問題に取り組むことにある。❷バクテリアからクジラまで、地球の全ての生物は潜在的に地球の健康にとって重要である。❸大きなクジラであろうが、小さなウィルスであろうが、いかなる生物の消滅も真剣に受けとめなければならない。なぜなら、それら全てに果たす役割があるからだ。❹地球からこれらの一つでも除去するなら、私達は自らの一部を破壊しているのだ。というのも、私達もまたガイアの一部であるからだ。❺エリザベス朝時代の詩人ジョン・ダンが言ったように、「そしてゆえに問うなかれ、誰がために鐘は鳴るのかと：それはそなたのために鳴る」。

5 ❶ガイア理論の支持者の間の主な懸念は、人間が惑星に持ちこたえることのできないストレスを課したため、私たちに有利にはたらく地球の自己調節能力が限界に到達しているかもしれないということだ。❷産業革命以降、人間の活動の副産物として発生した温暖化効果は氷河期の終わり以来の他のいかなる時期よりも高く気温を上昇させて、前世紀には上昇傾向が最大だった。❸もし二酸化炭素の放出が増え続ければ、2100年までに、地球の気温は人類が見たことのないようなレベルに到達するだろう。❹ガイアは新たな均衡を作り出して反応しなければならないだろう。❺この均衡が人間の生命維持と両立可能であることを希望するのみである。

*デイジーワールド：1983年ジェームズ・ラブロックとアンドリュー・ワトソンが発表したガイア理論の論文で紹介された白いデイジーと黒いデイジーだけが存在する仮想の惑星。

重要語句

☐ hypothesise that ...	〔動〕…だと仮説をたてる
☐ analogous to ...	〔形〕…に似ている ＝ similar to ...
☐ sustain ...	〔動〕…を維持する
☐ A is to B as (= what) C is to D	〔熟〕AとBの関係はCとDの関係と同じだ
☐ proliferate	〔動〕増殖する
☐ die off	〔動〕次々に死ぬ、絶滅する

☐ **in turn**	〔副〕順番に、今度は同様に
☐ **in one's favour**	〔熟〕の有利に
☐ **compatible with ...**	〔形〕…に一致して、…と両立可能な
☐ **proponent**	〔名〕支持者 = supporter

正解一覧

1 self-regulating	**2** body	**3** goddess
4 air	**5** AまたはE	**6** EまたはA
7 absorbing	**8** reflecting	**9** photosynthesis
10 outnumber	**11** FALSE	**12** NOT GIVEN
13 TRUE		

問題文和訳

Questions 1–4

要約を完成しなさい。

それぞれの解答を本文から1語だけ選んで、1–4の欄に記入しなさい。

ガイア理論によれば、地球の機能は **1** 自己調節する生物に類似している。多くの点で地球は生き延びるために必要な状況を維持する人間の **2** 身体に似ている。 ガイア理論は地球を象徴する **3** 女神にちなんで名づけられ、ラブロック博士は生態系の豊かなイメージを作り上げた。例えるならば、地球にとっての **4** 空気は猫にとっての毛皮である。

1 ┃正解┃ **self-regulating**
1段落3文に地球はa living organism that sustains the conditions suitable for its own survival（地球は自らの生存に適した状態を持続する生物）と似ているとあるが、that節の内容を1つの単語で言い換えたものとして同じ段落第1文のself-regulatingが妥当だ。

2 ┃正解┃ **body**
1段落2文が設問部分と該当している。後半の内容を確認すれば選択可能。

3 ┃正解┃ **goddess**
2段落1文後半が設問部分と同じ内容なので 'goddess' が空所に適合する。

4 ┃正解┃ **air**
2段落5文の比喩表現に相当する。問題中の構文A is to B what C is to D は

「BにとってのAは、DにとってのCと同じだ」の意味。

▌問題文和訳

Questions 5–6

A–Eから正しいものを2つ選び、解答用紙の5, 6の欄に記入しなさい。
解答はどの順序でも良い。
本文中で述べられている雲の形成のプロセスに影響を与える要素は以下のどの2つか？

> **A** 藻類の化学的プロセス
> **B** リン分子
> **C** 海洋潮
> **D** 動物の代謝
> **E** 余剰ガス

5 ┃正解┃ A または E
6 ┃正解┃ E または A

2段落3文に雲の形成の言及があり、大洋の藻類の代謝作用と排ガスの化学的プロセスについての記述はあるが、その他の記述はない。

▌問題文和訳

Questions 7–10

以下の文を完成させなさい。
それぞれの解答を本文から1語だけ選びなさい。
解答用紙の7–10の欄に解答を記入しなさい。

7 黒いデイジーの花びらは白いデイジーの花びらよりも太陽光を<u>吸収する</u>ことに優れている。
8 白いデイジーは太陽光線を効率的に<u>反射する</u>。
9 とても効率的に<u>光合成</u>を利用できることにより、黒いデイジーは寒い気候で繁茂する。
10 黒いデイジーは白いデイジー<u>よりも数が増える</u>につれて、デイジーワールドの気温は上昇する。

7 |正解| absorbing

3段落3文に黒いデイジーは白いデイジーよりも光を吸収するとある。

8 |正解| reflecting

3段落4文に白いデイジーはよく光を反射するとある。

9 |正解| photosynthesis

3段落10文に、黒いデイジーの寒い気温での優位な特徴として光合成について述べられている。

10 |正解| outnumber

3段落6文に、気温が上昇する理由として黒いデイジーが白いデイジーよりも増えることが言及されている。

問題文和訳

Questions 11–13

以下の文は本文に与えられた情報と一致するか？

解答用紙11–13の欄に…を記入しなさい。

TRUE	文が情報に一致すれば
FALSE	文が情報に矛盾すれば
NOT GIVEN	これについての情報がなければ

11 ガイア理論はジェームズ・ラブロックによって1960年代初頭に開発された。

12 地球上では、デイジーは2つの基本的な種類に分類できる。

13 私達はどんな生物の死も真剣に受けとめなければならない。

11 |正解| FALSE

2段落1文でThe Gaia theory was developed in the late 1960s（ガイア理論は1960年代後半に構築された）とあるので、1960年代初頭ではない。

12 |正解| NOT GIVEN

本文で黒と白のデイジーが例示として使用されているが、デイジーの植物本来としての分類の記述はない。

13 |正解| TRUE

4段落3文We must take seriously the death of any creature, whether a great whale or a tiny virus（大きなクジラであろうが、小さなウィルスであろうが、いかなる生物の消滅も真剣に受けとめなければならない）が同じ内容。organism「有機体、生物」とcreatureが同意であることに気づけば選択

できる。

*You should spend about 20 minutes on **Questions 1–13,** which are based on the reading passage below.*

Questions 1–5

The reading passage has seven paragraphs, **A–G**.

*Choose the correct heading for paragraphs **B–F** from the list of headings below.*

*Write the correct number, **i–vii**, in boxes 1–5 on your answer sheet.*

	List of Headings
i	Key components of the diet
ii	Some practical tips
iii	Taking care of your heart
iv	Choose your fat wisely
v	Reduced chance of disease
vi	A glass a day keeps the doctor away
vii	Lifestyle is also important

Example	Paragraph **A**	*Answer*	**iii**
1	Paragraph **B**		
2	Paragraph **C**		
3	Paragraph **D**		
4	Paragraph **E**		
5	Paragraph **F**		
Example	Paragraph **G**	*Answer*	**vii**

The Mediterranean Diet

A   The well-known saying 'An ounce of prevention beats a pound of cure' is never truer than when it applies to taking care of your heart. Heart disease is one of the major killers in our society, and the best way to make sure your heart functions well is to adopt a healthy diet. If you're looking for a heart-healthy eating plan, the Mediterranean diet is the way to go. The Mediterranean diet combines all the elements of healthy eating traditionally practised by people in the countries bordering the Mediterranean Sea. As a bonus, it's also delicious. No wonder Mediterranean villages always seem to be full of contented old people.

B   Research on national diets around the world has shown that the traditional Mediterranean diet reduces the risk of a wide range of diseases. A recent analysis of more than one million adults showed that a Mediterranean diet was associated with a reduced risk of cardiovascular illness, cancer, and Alzheimer's disease. For this reason, doctors are increasingly encouraging people to adopt a Mediterranean-style diet to minimise the risk of chronic diseases.

C   Fruits, vegetables, pasta and rice are a big part of the traditional Mediterranean diet. Residents of Greece eat very little red meat and eat, on average, nine servings a day of fruits and vegetables, which are rich in anti-oxidants. People on Mediterranean diets tend to have lower levels of LDL cholesterol, which is the "bad" cholesterol that builds up deposits in your arteries. Nuts are also an important part of a healthy Mediterranean diet. Although 80 percent of a nut's calories come from fat, most of this fat is unsaturated, which is much healthier than saturated fat. The grains eaten in the Mediterranean region are generally whole grains, containing few unhealthy trans fats, and bread is an important part of the diet. When bread is eaten, it is dipped in olive oil, not smeared with butter or margarine, which tends to be high in trans fats.

D Eating too much fat can be a killer, but the Mediterranean diet is more about making wise choices about the types of fat you eat rather than limiting total fat consumption. The typical Mediterranean diet contains low levels of the saturated fats and trans fats that can contribute to heart disease. The primary source of fat in a Mediterranean diet is olive oil, which provides healthier monounsaturated fats. Nuts are also an important source of healthy fats. Some nuts contain omega-3 fatty acids, which decrease blood clotting, lower the risk of sudden heart attack, improve the health of blood vessels, and regulate blood pressure. Many types of fish, such as mackerel, herring, and sardines, are also rich sources of omega-3 fatty acids, and fish is eaten on a regular basis in a Mediterranean diet.

E While the health benefits of alcohol are controversial, and doctors are hesitant about encouraging alcohol consumption because of the dangers of excessive drinking, the truth is that a moderate intake of alcohol has been associated with a reduced risk of heart disease in some studies. The Mediterranean diet typically includes a moderate amount of wine, generally about a glass a day. Although more than this may increase the chance of health problems, including an increased risk of certain types of cancer, sensible drinking habits can further enhance the benefits of a Mediterranean diet.

F Arguably the best thing about the Mediterranean diet is that it is incredibly delicious, so there is no downside. If you aim to switch to this diet, bear in mind the following:
- Most of your meals should involve an abundance of minimally processed plant foods. Ideally, you should eat seven to ten servings a day of fruit and vegetables, switch to whole-grain bread and cereal, and eat plenty of whole-grain rice, beans and pasta products.
- Keep nuts handy around the house for quick snacks. Almonds, cashews and walnuts are ideal, and sesame seeds are handy

additions to many salads. Try to eat them every day.

· As often as you can, replace butter or margarine with olive oil. After cooking pasta, add olive oil, garlic and onions for flavouring. Dip your bread in flavoured olive oil as a tasty alternative to butter.

· Season your meals with healthy herbs and spices rather than salt.

· Try to eat fish at least once a week. Remember to grill your fish rather than fry it.

· Avoid red meat, eating chicken as a replacement whenever you can. Also avoid sausage, bacon and other high-fat meats.

· Limit dairy products, cheese and ice cream, although you can enjoy these foods occasionally.

· Drink a glass of wine at dinner. If you are not comfortable with the idea of drinking alcohol, you can enjoy a glass of fresh grape juice instead.

G   Finally, it should be remembered that health and longevity is not all about diet. Mediterranean people traditionally enjoy being a part of large social groups, walk a lot, and live low-stress lives. These may all be just as important to a long life as a good diet. As a recipe for health, long life, and happiness, the best advice is to combine a good diet with a good lifestyle.

Questions 6–8

Label the pyramid below.

*Fill in **TWO** types of food for each of the categories **A**, **B**, and **C** from among the list below.*

Write in boxes 6–8 on your answer sheet.

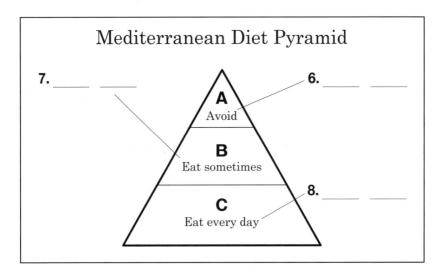

Mediterranean Diet Pyramid

7. _____ _____

6. _____ _____

A
Avoid

B
Eat sometimes

8. _____ _____

C
Eat every day

| cheese | nuts | yoghurt | sausage | butter | fruit |
| vegetables | ice cream | beans | bacon | olive oil | |

Questions 9–13

Do the following statements reflect the opinion of the writer in the reading passage?

In boxes 9–13 of your answer sheet, write

YES   if the statement reflects the opinion of the writer
NO   if the statement contradicts the opinion of the writer
NOT GIVEN   if it is impossible to say what the writer thinks about
                this

9   The Mediterranean diet is one of many fashionable diets.
10 A study of 100,000 people proved that a Mediterranean diet is healthy.
11 The Mediterranean diet emphasises limiting fat consumption.
12 Some nuts help to control blood pressure.
13 Drinking moderate amounts of wine can improve a person's health.

| 解答解説

全文訳

地中海式食生活

A ❶「1オンスの予防は1ポンドの治療に値する（転ばぬ先の杖）」という有名なことわざは、心臓のケアにあてはめた時ほど真実味が増すことはない。❷心臓病は我々の社会で主要な死因の1つで、確実に心臓を機能させる最善の方法は健康的な食生活を取り入れることだ。❸もしあなたが心臓に良い献立を探しているのなら、地中海式食生活がうってつけだ。❹地中海式食生活は、地中海に隣接する国々の人々が伝統的に実践している健康的な食事法のすべての要素を組み合わせたものだ。❺おまけに美味しいのだ。❻地中海の村にはいつも幸せな高齢者であふれているように見えるのも不思議ではない。

B ❶世界中の国民食の調査で、伝統的な地中海式食生活が様々な病気のリスクを減らすことが示されている。❷100万人以上の成人を対象とした最近の分析では、地中海式食生活が心臓血管疾患、癌、アルツハイマー病のリスクの軽減につながることがわかった。❸このような理由で、慢性病のリスクを最小限にするため、医者はますます人々に地中海式食生活の採用を奨励している。

C ❶果物、野菜、パスタ、米が伝統的な地中海式食生活で大きな割合を占める。❷ギリシャの住民はほとんど赤身の肉を食べず、平均して1日9皿の果物と野菜を食べるが、それらは抗酸化物質が豊富である。❸地中海式食生活をとる人々はLDLコレステロール、つまり動脈内に沈着する「悪玉」コレステロールのレベルが低い傾向がある。❹木の実も健康的な地中海式食生活の重要な部分だ。❺木の実のカロリーの80パーセントは脂肪だが、その大半は不飽和であり、飽和脂肪よりずっと健康的だ。❻地中海地域で食べられている穀物は一般的に全粒粉で、不健康なトランス脂肪をほとんど含まない。そして、パンもこの食事の中で重要な位置付けだ。❼パンが食べられる時、トランス脂肪が高い傾向のあるバターやマーガリンが塗られるのではなく、オリーブオイルに浸される。

D ❶脂肪の食べ過ぎは致命的だが、地中海式食生活は総脂肪消費量を制限するよりも、むしろ食べる脂肪のタイプについて賢明な選択をする。❷典型的な地中海式食生活は、心臓病の一因となる可能性のある飽和脂肪とトランス脂肪の値が低い。❸地中海式食生活の主な脂肪源はオリーブオイルで、より健康的な一価不飽和脂肪

を供給する。❹木の実も健康的な脂肪の重要な供給源である。❺中にはオメガ３脂肪酸を含むものもあり、血液凝固を減らし、突然の心臓発作のリスクを下げ、血管の健康状態を改善し、血圧を調整する。❻サバ、ニシン、イワシのような多くの種類の魚もオメガ３脂肪酸の宝庫で、地中海式食生活では魚が日常的に食べられる。

E ❶アルコールの健康への効果には議論の余地があり、過剰な飲酒の危険性があるため医者はアルコールの摂取をすすめるのに躊躇する。しかし、実際のところ、いくつかの研究で適度なアルコールの摂取は心臓病のリスクの軽減につながるという結果が出ている。❷地中海式食生活は典型的にほどほどの量のワインを含み、大抵は１日グラス１杯である。❸これ以上になると、特定の種類の癌のリスクの増加を含め、健康問題の発生の危険が高まるかもしれないが、節度ある飲酒習慣が地中海式食生活の効果をさらに高めている可能性がある。

F ❶ほぼ間違いなく地中海式食生活が優れている点は、非常に美味しいということであり、否定的な側面がない。❷もしこの食生活に切り替えるつもりなら、以下のことに留意すべきだ。

・❸ほとんどの食事で、加工を最小限にとどめた植物性食品をたっぷり摂るべきだ。❹理想的には、１日７〜10皿の果物と野菜を食べると良い。全粒パン、全粒シリアルに切り替えるべきだ。たくさんの玄米、豆類と全粒パスタ製品をたくさん食べなさい。

・❺木の実を手軽なスナック用に家に常備しておきなさい。❻アーモンド、カシューナッツ、くるみが理想的で、胡麻はサラダの手頃な調味料として重宝する。❼毎日食べるようにしなさい。

・❽できるだけバターとマーガリンをオリーブオイルに換えなさい。❾パスタを茹でたら、オリーブオイル、にんにく、たまねぎを風味づけに加えなさい。❿バターの美味しい代用品として、風味をつけたオリーブオイルにパンを浸しなさい。

・⓫塩よりも健康的なハーブか香辛料で食事の風味づけをするようにしなさい。

・⓬少なくとも週一回は魚を食べるようにしなさい。⓭忘れずにフライではなくグリルにしなさい。

・⓮赤肉を避けて、そのかわり可能な限り鶏肉を食べなさい。⓯また、ソーセージ、ベーコンなどの高脂肪の肉は避けなさい。

・⓰乳製品、チーズとアイスクリームは制限しなさい。しかし、時々ならばこれらの食品を楽しんでも良い。

・⓱夕食時にグラス１杯のワインを飲みなさい。⓲もし快くアルコールを飲む気になれないのなら、かわりに１杯の新鮮な葡萄ジュースを味わうのも良い。

G ❶最後に、健康と長寿は食事が全てではないことを覚えておくべきである。❷地中海の人々は伝統的に大きな社会集団に属することを楽しみとして、たくさん歩き、ストレスの少ない生活を送る。❸こうしたこと全てが良い食生活と同じくらい長寿にとって大切なのかもしれないのだ。❹健康、長寿、幸福のレシピとしての最高の助言は、身体に良い食事と良いライフスタイルを同時に行うことだ。

重要語句

□ **the way to go**	〔熟〕断然よい《way to go「よくやった。その調子だ」》
□ **cardiovascular**	〔形〕心臓血管の
□ **chronic**	〔形〕慢性の ⇔ acute「急性の」
□ **artery**	〔名〕動脈
□ **saturated**	〔形〕飽和した
□ **blood vessels**	〔名〕血管
□ **moderate**	〔形〕節度のある、適量の
□ **arguably**	〔副〕ほぼ間違いなく
□ **bear … in mind**	〔熟〕…を心に留める
□ **alternative**	〔名〕代替案

正解一覧

1 v 　**2** i 　**3** iv 　**4** vi 　**5** ii

6 sausage / butter / bacon （いずれか2つ）

7 cheese / yoghurt / ice cream （いずれか2つ）

8 nuts / fruit / vegetables / beans / olive oil （いずれか2つ）

9 NOT GIVEN 　**10** NO 　**11** NO 　**12** YES 　**13** YES

問題文和訳

Questions 1–5

本文はA–Gの7段落である。下の見出しリストから段落B–Fの正しい見出しを選びなさい。

解答用紙の1–5の欄にi–viiを記入しなさい。

	見出しのリスト
i	食事の重要な要素

ii	いくつかの実用的な秘訣		
iii	心臓のケアをすること		
iv	脂肪を賢く選ぶ		
v	発病リスクの減少		
vi	グラス1杯が医者を遠ざける		
vii	ライフスタイルもまた重要である		

例	**A**段落	解答	iii
1	**B**段落		
2	**C**段落		
3	**D**段落		
4	**E**段落		
5	**F**段落		
例	**G**段落	解答	vii

1 |正解| v

B段落1文Research on national diets around the world has shown that the traditional Mediterranean diet reduces the risk of a wide range of diseases.（世界中の国民食の調査で、伝統的な地中海式食生活は幅広い範囲の病気のリスクを減らすことが示されている）に病気のリスクの減少が、2文には具体的な病名cardiovascular illness, cancer, and Alzheimer's disease（心臓の血管疾患、癌、アルツハイマー病）の記述がある。

2 |正解| i

C段落1文に「食生活の重要な部分」とあり、地中海式食生活で使用する食材と栄養面の言及がある。

3 |正解| iv

D段落1文に「食べる脂肪のタイプについて賢明な選択」とある。

4 |正解| vi

E段落はアルコールが主題で、1〜2文に「適量＝1日グラス1杯」と「心臓病のリスクの軽減」が結びつくとある。"適度な量"が重要なので、vだけでは正解にはならない。

5 |正解| ii

F段落には全部で8つの秘訣が述べられている。

Questions 6–8

ピラミッドに分類しなさい。以下のリストからA, B, Cのカテゴリーそれぞれにあてはまる食品を2つ選んで、解答用紙6–8の欄に記入しなさい。

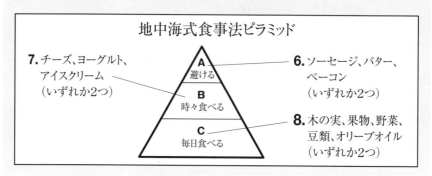

地中海式食事法ピラミッド

7. チーズ、ヨーグルト、アイスクリーム（いずれか2つ）

A 避ける
B 時々食べる
C 毎日食べる

6. ソーセージ、バター、ベーコン（いずれか2つ）

8. 木の実、果物、野菜、豆類、オリーブオイル（いずれか2つ）

| チーズ | 木の実 | ヨーグルト | ソーセージ | バター | 果物 |
| 野菜 | アイスクリーム | 豆類 | ベーコン | オリーブオイル | |

6 |正解| sausage, butter, bacon （いずれか2つ）

F段落の2文bear in mind the following（以下のことに留意すべき）とあり、秘訣が言及されている。3つ目の秘訣の「できるだけバターをオリーブオイルに換えなさい」から、バターには否定的なのでAに入れる。6つ目に「ソーセージ、ベーコンなどの高脂肪の肉は避けなさい」の記述がある。

7 |正解| cheese, yoghurt, ice cream （いずれか2つ）

7つ目の秘訣としてLimit dairy products, cheese and ice cream, although you can enjoy these foods occasionally（乳製品、チーズとアイスクリームは制限しなさい。しかし、時々ならばこれらの食品を楽しんでも良い）と述べられている。

8 |正解| nuts, fruit, vegetables, beans, olive oil （いずれか2つ）

F段落で毎日食べるものとして果物、野菜、木の実、豆類等が列挙され、オリーブオイルについては3つ目の秘訣に記されているほか、D段落に利点が言及されており、3文目のThe primary source of fat is olive oil（主な脂肪源はオリーブオイル）の記述からCに入れるのが妥当。

問題文和訳

Questions 9–13

以下の文章は本文の筆者の意見を反映しているか？
解答用紙の9–13欄に以下のいずれかを書きなさい。

YES　　　　筆者の主張と一致している
NO　　　　筆者の主張に矛盾する
NOT GIVEN　このことについての筆者の考えが述べられていない

9　地中海式食生活は多くの流行りの食生活の1つだ。
10　10万人を対象とした調査は、地中海式食生活が健康的であることを証明した。
11　地中海式食生活は脂肪消費を制限することを強調する。
12　木の実のなかには血圧を抑えるのに役立つものもある。
13　適量のワインを飲むと健康を高める可能性がある。

9 正解 NOT GIVEN
B段落1文に国民食や伝統的な食生活の言及はあるが、流行の食生活という記述は見当たらない。

10 正解 NO
B段落2文はmore than one million（100万人より多い）を指すので数字の誤り。英数字thousand, million, billionの数え方は、特に0の数がいくつであるか整理しておくと良い。

11 正解 NO
D段落1文にthe Mediterranean diet is more about making wise choices about the types of fat you eat …（地中海式食生活は食べる脂肪のタイプについて賢明な選択をする…）とあるので誤り。

12 正解 YES
D段落5文にSome nuts contain omega-3 fatty acids, which decrease blood clotting … and regulate blood pressure（中にはオメガ3脂肪酸を含むものもあり、血液凝固を減らし、突然の心臓発作のリスクを下げ、血管の健康状態を改善し、血圧を調整する）とある。

13 正解 YES
E段落1文の後半にa moderate intake of alcohol has been associated with a reduced risk of heart disease（適度なアルコールの摂取は心臓病のリスクの軽減につながる）とあり、正しいと言える。

*You should spend about 20 minutes on **Questions 1–13,** which are based on the reading passage below.*

The Coffee House

Coffee is one of the world's most popular beverages, and drinking coffee in a café, or coffee shop, is deeply ingrained in many cultures. We take it for granted that we can find a café pretty much anywhere we happen to be, whether in our home towns or in a city on the other side of the world. Cafés may be havens of peace or hubs of lively chatter; they may simply offer a drink and a place to sit down, or come replete with shelves of books, sofas and classical music. To be sure, they have diversified in countless ways since their earliest appearance in the days of the Ottoman Empire.

The Turks have a long tradition of drinking coffee in their homes, and from the 16th century onward public coffee houses began to appear in the empire's capital of Istanbul. Soon they spread to Cairo and other parts of the Ottoman Empire, although they were not always welcome. Coffee houses in Mecca were banned by imams (Moslem religious leaders) as they became places for undesirable political gatherings. In the 17th century, traffic between the Ottoman Empire and neighbouring European countries helped coffee houses to spread westward, and they were soon established in Vienna, Paris and London.

The traditional tale of the origins of the Viennese café begins with sacks of mysterious green beans being left behind by the Turks when they retreated after the Battle of Vienna in 1683. According to this story, one of the king's officers had experience of living in Turkey, and he used the beans to establish the first Viennese coffee house. However, historians now believe this tale to be false, and it is widely accepted that the first coffee house in Vienna was actually opened by a Greek merchant. The first café in Paris appeared in 1672, and coffee houses became major meeting places of the French Enlightenment. One such place, frequented by Voltaire, Rousseau and Diderot, arguably gave birth to the first modern encyclopedia. America had its first coffee house in Boston in 1676.

In England, coffee houses originally appeared in the city of Oxford, and as they proliferated in this scholarly town they earned a reputation as places for intellectual debate. Topics discussed included politics and scandal, current events, and the natural sciences. Historians often view English coffee houses during the 17th and 18th centuries in the context of the Age of Enlightenment, when reasoned debate took over from deference to religious and political authority. The coffee houses became known as 'penny universities' (typically, a penny purchased a cup of coffee and admission) as they catered to a range of learning, including lessons in French, Italian, Latin, dancing, fencing and mathematics.

One reason for the popularity of English coffee houses is that they were bastions of democratic speech where men of any station in life could enter. According to the first posted 'Rules and Orders of the Coffee House' printed in 1674, equality prevailed in these establishments, and 'no man of any station need give his place to a finer man'. The same document included the rules that anyone who swore would have to forfeit a shilling, and if an argument broke out, the one who started it would have to buy the other party a cup of coffee.

Coffee shops in the United States arose from the espresso and pastry-centred coffee houses of the Italian-American communities in the major U.S. cities, notably New York and San Francisco. From the late 1950s onward, coffee houses also served as venues for folk music performers, and the poets and authors of the Beat movement spent a great deal of time there. In the 1960s, Joan Baez, Bob Dylan, and other singers used coffee houses as venues to experiment with fusing folk and rock music, and it could be said that these places launched their careers. America also saw the birth of the café chain Starbucks, which has taken the world by storm with its comfortable seating, gourmet coffee served by knowledgeable baristas and Wi-Fi (wireless internet access) hotspots at no charge. This rebranding of the coffee house, now known more commonly as a 'coffee shop,' for the modern consumer has helped to recreate it in a trendy image for today's youth.

Questions 1–5

Look at the following statements and the list of cities below.
Match each statement with the correct city, **A–E**.
Write the correct letter **A–E** in boxes 1–5 on your answer sheet.

1   The city that probably inspired the first encyclopedia.
2   The place where coffee shops promoted scientific debate and
diverse learning.
3   The city which saw coffee shops closed down for spreading
dangerous ideas.
4   The place where people of Italian ancestry proved instrumental in
spreading the coffee culture.
5   The city in which a Greek merchant is thought to have established
the first coffee house.

List of Cities	
A	Mecca
B	Vienna
C	Paris
D	Oxford
E	San Francisco

Questions 6–10

Do the following statements agree with the information given in the reading passage?

In boxes 6–10 on your answer sheet, write

> **TRUE**   *if the statement agrees with the information*
> **FALSE**   *if the statement contradicts the information*
> **NOT GIVEN**   *if there is no information on this*

6   Coffee drinking spread eastwards from Europe to the Ottoman Empire.

7   Historians believe Vienna discovered coffee thanks to beans left after an attack.

8   The English coffee house usually cost a penny for entry and a drink.

9   Foreign languages could be studied in some coffee houses.

10 Picasso and Hemingway frequented Parisian cafés.

Questions 11–13

*Choose the correct letter, **A**, **B**, **C** or **D**.*

Write your answers in boxes 11–13 on your answer sheet.

11 According to the passage, what did English and French coffee houses have in common?

    A They imported coffee beans from the Ottoman Empire.

    B They played a part in the Age of Enlightenment.

    C They were established by the 16th century.

    D Their customers had to follow strict rules.

12 What was the most important factor behind the popularity of English coffee houses of the 17th and 18th centuries?

    A The opportunity to attend university for a penny

    B The facts that all patrons were treated as equals

    C The rules and fines for people who swore

    D The rules that encouraged strong arguments

13 How did coffee shops prove conducive to the spread of American counter- culture?

    A They allowed students to conduct social experiments.

    B They ushered in the birth of coffee fusion drinks.

    C They exposed promising young performers to a wider audience.

    D They provided comfortable seating and gourmet coffee.

第2章

Exercise

NO TEST MATERIAL ON THIS PAGE

コーヒーハウス

1 ❶ コーヒーは世界で最も人気のある飲み物の1つで、カフェやコーヒー店でコーヒーを飲むことが多くの文化に深く根づいている。❷ 地元の町であれ地球の反対側の町であれ、たまたま居合わせた所ならほとんどどこにでもカフェを見つけられることが、私達には当たり前になっている。❸ カフェは平和な避難場所、活発なおしゃべりの拠点であるかもしれない。カフェは単に飲み物と座る場所を提供するだけのこともあれば、本棚やソファを備えクラシック音楽が聞こえてくることもあるかもしれない。❹ 確かに、カフェはオスマン帝国の時代の最初期の出現から、数えきれないくらい多様化してきた。

2 ❶ トルコ人は家でコーヒーを飲む長い伝統があり、16世紀以降、帝国の首都イスタンブールにコーヒーハウスが出現し始めた。❷ 間もなくカイロやオスマン帝国の他の地域に拡がったが、常に歓迎されたわけではなかった。❸ メッカのコーヒーハウスは、望ましくない政治集会の場所になったので、イマーム（イスラム教の宗教指導者）によって禁止された。❹ 17世紀、オスマン帝国とヨーロッパの近隣諸国の間の交通のおかげで、コーヒーハウスは西に拡がり、間もなくウィーン、パリ、ロンドンにもできた。

3 ❶ ウィーンのカフェの起源について伝えられている話は、1683年第2次ウィーン包囲*の後トルコ人が退却した時に謎めいた緑色の豆の袋が置き去りにされていたことに始まる。❷ この話によれば、王軍*の1人がトルコに住んだ経験があり、その豆を使って最初のウィンナーコーヒーの店を創業した。❸ しかし、歴史家は現在この話を嘘だと考えており、ウィーン初のコーヒーハウスは実際のところギリシャの商人によって開店されたのだという説が広く受け入れられている。❹ パリ初のカフェは1672年に登場し、コーヒーハウスはフランス啓蒙運動の主な集会場所となった。❺ おそらく、こうした店の1つにヴォルテール、ルソー、ディドロが頻繁に訪れ、初の近代百科事典が制作された。❻ アメリカでは1676年ボストンに初のコーヒーハウスができた。

4 ❶ イングランドでは、コーヒーハウスは初めオクスフォードの町に登場し、この学問の町で急増するにつれて、知的な討論の場所として評判になった。❷ 論じられる話題は、政治、スキャンダル、時事問題、自然科学だった。❸ 歴史家はしばしば、17世紀、18世紀の英国のコーヒーハウスを啓蒙思想の時代背景の中で捉えるが、宗教や政治的権

威への服従から離れて理性的思考の議論が始まった時代だった。❹コーヒーハウスは、フランス語、イタリア語、ラテン語、ダンス、フェンシング、数学のレッスンを含む幅広い学問の需要に応えたので「ペニー大学」（一般的にコーヒー1杯と入場料で1ペニーだった）として知られるようになった。

5　❶英国でコーヒーハウスが人気だった理由の1つは、どんな身分の男性でも入ることができる民主主義的な議論の拠点だったからだ。❷初めて掲示された1674年印刷の「コーヒーハウスのルールと命令」によれば、これらの施設には平等原理が行き届き、「どんな身分の男性も自分より位の高い人に場所を譲る必要はない」とあった。❸その同じ文書には、悪態をついた人は1シリング没収される、もし口論が勃発したら始めた人が相手にコーヒーを1杯おごらなければならないというルールも含まれていた。

6　❶アメリカ合衆国のコーヒー店は、大都市、特にニューヨークとサン・フランシスコのイタリア系アメリカ人社会のエスプレッソとペストリー中心のコーヒーハウスから生まれた。❷1950年後半以降、コーヒーハウスはフォーク音楽の演奏者のライブ会場の役目も果たし、ビート運動*の詩人や著者が多くの時間をそこで過ごした。❸1960年代、ジョーン・バエズ、ボブ・ディランのような歌手がフォーク音楽とロック音楽を実験的に融合させるライブ会場としてコーヒーハウスを利用し、こうした場所で彼らがミュージシャンとしてのキャリアを歩み始めたと言うこともできる。❹アメリカではコーヒーチェーン店スターバックスも誕生し、快適な座席、知識のあるバリスタが淹れるグルメ・コーヒー、無料のWi-Fi（無線のインターネットアクセス）のホットスポットで世界に旋風を巻き起こした。❺現在一般的にコーヒーショップとして知られるようになっているが、現代の消費者のためのコーヒーハウスのこのようなブランド再生化は、今日の若者向けの流行のイメージで生まれ変わることに役立った。

*第二次ウィーン包囲：1683年のオスマン帝国によるウィーンへの進撃
*王軍：オスマン帝国に対抗していたポーランド・リトアニア共和国の軍
*ビート運動：1950年代のアメリカで起きた支配的、保守的文化や体制に反抗した運動

重要語句

☐ **take it for granted that …**	〔熟〕…を当然と思う	
☐ **replete with ...**	〔形〕…でいっぱいの ＝ filled with ...	
☐ **retreat ...**	〔動〕…から撤退する	
☐ **frequent ...**	〔動〕…に頻繁に訪れる	
☐ **context**	〔名〕背景状況、文脈	
☐ **take over**	〔動〕…を引き継ぐ	

☐ prevail			〔動〕普及する					
☐ forfeit ...			〔動〕…を失う、…を没収される					
☐ venue for ...			〔名〕…の開催地、現場					
☐ take ... by storm			〔熟〕…を圧倒する					

正解一覧

1 C	**2** D	**3** A	**4** E	**5** B
6 FALSE	**7** FALSE	**8** TRUE	**9** TRUE	
10 NOT GIVEN	**11** B	**12** B	**13** C	

問題文和訳

Questions 1–5

以下の記述と都市のリストを見なさい。

それぞれの記述とA–Eの正しい都市を結びつけなさい。

解答用紙1–5の欄にA–Eの正しいものを記入しなさい。

1 おそらく最初の百科事典が作られるきっかけとなった都市。

2 科学に関する討論と多様な学びを奨励するコーヒー店がある場所。

3 危険な考えを広めたとしてコーヒー店が閉鎖された都市。

4 コーヒー文化を広めるのにイタリア系の人々が重要な役割を果たした場所。

5 ギリシャの商人が最初のコーヒーハウスを創業した考えられる都市。

> **都市のリスト**
> **A** メッカ
> **B** ウィーン
> **C** パリ
> **D** オクスフォード
> **E** サン・フランシスコ

1 ┃正解┃ C

3段落5文で百科事典の誕生について言及されている。

2 |正解| **D**
4段落1～2文から、コーヒーハウスが知的な議論の場で、自然科学が話題の
1つだったことがわかる。

3 |正解| **A**
2段落3文に「政治集会の場だったために禁止された」とある。

4 |正解| **E**
6段落1文に「イタリア系アメリカ人社会」とある。

5 |正解| **B**
3段落3文に同じ内容の言及がある。

問題文和訳

Questions 6–10

以下の文は本文に与えられた情報と一致するか？
解答用紙6–10の欄内に…を書きなさい。

TRUE	もし文が情報に一致していれば
FALSE	もし文が情報に矛盾していれば
NOT GIVEN	もしこれに関しての情報がなければ

6   コーヒーを飲む習慣はヨーロッパからオスマン帝国へ東に拡がった。

7   歴史家たちは攻撃の後に残された豆のおかげでウィーンがコーヒーを発
見したのだと信じている。

8   英国のコーヒーハウスは入店と飲み物代にたいてい1ペニーかかった。

9   外国語を学ぶことができるコーヒーハウスがあった。

10 ピカソやヘミングウェーはパリのカフェを頻繁に訪れた。

6 |正解| FALSE
2段落4文に「オスマン帝国からヨーロッパへ西に拡がった」とあるので方
向が逆。

7 |正解| FALSE
3段落1～2文で、トルコに住んだ経験がある（←コーヒーを知っていた）人
がその豆で店を始めたという言い伝えが述べられ、3文で「歴史家はこの話
を嘘だと考えている」とあるので「信じている」は誤り。

8 |正解| TRUE
4段落4文に「ペニー大学」と呼ばれた経緯として同様の記述あり。

9 |正解| **TRUE**

4段落4文に仏、伊、ラテン語のレッスンの記述がある。

10 |正解| **NOT GIVEN**

ピカソ、ヘミングウェーについての記述はない。

|問題文和訳|

Questions 11–13

正しいものをA, B, C, Dから選び、解答用紙の11–13の欄に解答を記入しなさい。

11 本文によれば、英国とフランスのコーヒーハウスの共通点は何だったか？

  A オスマン帝国からコーヒー豆を輸入した。

  B 啓蒙時代に役割を果たした。

  C 16世紀までに創業された。

  D 客は厳しいルールを守らなければならなかった。

12 17世紀と18世紀に英国のコーヒーハウスが人気だった最も重要な要因は何か。

  A 1ペニーで大学に出席する機会

  B 全てのお客は平等に扱われたという事実

  C 乱暴な口をきく人々を対象とした規則と罰金

  D 激しい議論を促した規則

13 どのようにコーヒーハウスがアメリカの反体制文化の広がりに貢献したといえるか。

  A 学生が社会的実験を行えるようにした。

  B コーヒーを混ぜた飲み物の誕生の先駆けとなった。

  C 前途有望な若い演奏者を広く聴衆に知らしめた。

  D 座り心地の良い椅子とグルメ・コーヒーを提供した。

11 |正解| **B**

3段落4文にフランスの啓蒙運動、4段落3文に英国の啓蒙時代の言及があり、どちらの場合も、コーヒーハウスが知的な思想、または学問を啓発する場となったことが述べられている。

12 |正解| B

英国のコーヒーハウスについては4段落でも説明されているが、5段落でその人気の理由として誰でも入店できたこと平等原理に基づいたルールが言及されている。Cは最も重要な要因とは言えない。

13 |正解| C

最終段落2文、3文でアメリカにおける1950年～1960年代の既存の体制に対抗するフォーク、ロックなどの音楽シーンがコーヒーハウスの場を活用した記述がある。従ってCが正解。

第2章　解答解説

*You should spend about 20 minutes on **Questions 1–13,** which are based on the reading passage below.*

3D Printing: The Next Industrial Revolution

3D printing is a process of making a three-dimensional object by depositing layers of material in different shapes using digital technology. It is sometimes known as 'additive printing', which is distinct from traditional machining techniques that rely on removing material by methods such as cutting or drilling (subtractive processes). 3D printing has been around since the 1970s, but for long periods its use was confined to prototype parts to aid the design process. Now it is involved in the manufacturing stage in engineering, aerospace, and many other fields.

Printing in 3D is similar to clicking on the print button on a computer screen and sending a digital file to an inkjet printer. The difference is that instead of ink, a 3D printer deposits material in successive layers until a solid object emerges. The layers are put together in a number of ways. One of these spreads powder onto a tray and then solidifies it in the required pattern by sintering (applying heat) with a laser or an electron beam. Another method deposits filaments of molten plastic. After each layer is complete the build tray is lowered by a fraction of a millimetre and the next layer added. One great advantage of 3D printing is that it is a WYSIWYG ('what you see is what you get') process where the model you create on the computer screen is almost identical to the printed end product.

For more than a decade, 3D printers have been used as a means to make prototypes quickly and cheaply before the manufacturer begins the expensive business of tooling up a factory to produce the real thing. But the printers are evolving fast, and now more than 20% of 3D printer output is used to create final products. The printers themselves have been developed for rapid printing, with several machines now using multiple extruder heads, thus increasing overall print speed. Each multi-head machine can easily be reprogrammed, which opens the way to high-value-added 'mass customisation'.

An example that proves more than any other that 3D printing is coming of age is its use in building airplane parts. 3D printers are now used to print titanium landing-gear brackets that would normally have to be created out of a solid block of metal, and ultimately manufacturers hope to print the entire engine of an airplane. 3D printing could become especially important in aircraft manufacture because it is good at producing lightweight pieces. Even a small aircraft contains several tonnes of expensive titanium. These parts are usually machined from solid pieces of metal, which can result in 90% of the material being cut away. To make the same part with 3D printing, the printer spreads a layer of titanium powder about 20-30 microns (0.02–0.03mm) thick onto a tray, which it then fuses with lasers. There is almost no waste, and the parts can be easily optimised for their purpose, often coming out lighter but just as strong as conventionally manufactured parts. This is important because lightness is critical in making aircraft more fuel efficient. 3D manufacturing can thus help build more environmentally friendly aircraft.

3D printers also have the potential to transform manufacturing by lowering costs and risks. With lower costs, a producer no longer needs to make thousands of items to recover an investment, and this reduces the barriers to entry that were traditionally overcome only through economies of scale. The printers will also be ideally suited as a production method for 'mass customisation'. This is indeed already becoming reality, with some printing services allowing individuals to upload their own designs and have them manufactured by 3D printers.

As 3D printing technology improves and becomes more mainstream, the economic processes of making customised components will change dramatically, and we will soon see the emergence of the 'digital production plant'. A company needing a specialised part may find it cheaper and quicker to have that part printed locally or even to print its own rather than order one from a supplier based in another country. The inference is that some manufacturing will return to the West from cheap centres of production in China and elsewhere. Although Chinese companies are also adopting 3D printing technologies, in the future the cost of shipping the products could outweigh the cost of making them locally. This could help boost Western economies as they begin to bring manufacturing home.

Perhaps the most exciting aspect of 3D printing is that it offers a cheaper, less risky route to the market than the traditional one of setting up a factory or asking a mass-producer to make something. An entrepreneur can run off a few samples with a 3D printer to see if an idea works, and make a few more to see if the products are likely to sell. If the product is a success, then the business can scale up production. As a result, future success in manufacturing may depend less on scale and more on the quality of ideas. The downside is that good ideas can be copied even more rapidly with 3D printing than with conventional manufacturing, so battles over intellectual property rights may intensify.

The coming ubiquity of 3D printing throws up other fears for the future. In 2013 Cody Wilson, a law student at the University of Texas, leased time on 3D printers in order to produce, then successfully test, a plastic 30-round magazine for a popular type of rifle. This has led to fears that the new 3D printing technologies could be used for dangerous purposes. The United States already has a law banning guns that cannot be detected by common X-ray machines, but if the technology improves to the stage where anyone with a 3D printer can make their own firearms, then it may be necessary to rethink the legal framework for the regulation of these printing devices.

Questions 1–5

Do the following statements agree with the information given in the reading passage?

In boxes 1–5 on your answer sheet, write

TRUE	*if the statement agrees with the information*
FALSE	*if the statement contradicts the information*
NOT GIVEN	*if there is no information on this*

1   3D printing relies on a subtractive process to create new objects.
2   It is only recently that 3D printing has been used to create prototypes.
3   One advantage of using 3D printing is that less titanium is lost in the manufacturing process.
4   3D printing technology is more likely to succeed in the West than elsewhere.
5   Entrepreneurs will benefit from ongoing developments in 3D printing.

Questions 6–9

Complete each sentence with the correct ending, A–F, below.
Write the correct letter A–F in boxes 6–9 on your answer sheet.

6   After each layer of plastic is applied, the tray
7   More than one-fifth of 3D printer output
8   3D printing is useful in aircraft production as it
9   As production costs drop, a company

> **A**   is used to manufacture final products.
> **B**   can now manufacture a complete jet engine.
> **C**   is lowered to allow the next layer to be added.
> **D**   may shift its manufacturing back to the West.
> **E**   no longer requires programming skills.
> **F**   can produce lightweight components.

Questions 10–13

Complete the table below.

*Choose **NO MORE THAN THREE WORDS** from the reading passage for each answer.*

Write your answers in boxes 10–13 on your answer sheet.

The benefits and dangers of 3D printing	
Pros	- As the acronym **10** _____ suggests, you can print exactly what you see on the computer screen. - By eliminating the need for **11** _____, barriers to entry are likely to drop.
Cons	- The ease of copying designs will result in more arguments over **12** _____. - A real security threat is the danger of people manufacturing their own **13** _____.

Exercise 07 解答解説

全文訳

3Dプリント：次の産業革命

1 ❶3Dプリントはデジタル技術を使って異なる形に材質の層を積層させることによって3次元の物体を作る工程である。❷時として「積層印刷法」とも呼ばれるが、切ったり穴をあけたりするような方法（減法工程）によって材質を除去することに依存していた従来の機械加工技術と異なっている。❸3Dプリントは1970年代頃から存在していたが、その使用は長い間設計過程を補助するための試作部品に限られていた。❹現在、工学、航空宇宙産業、その他の多くの分野の製造段階に関わっている。

2 ❶3Dで印刷することは、コンピューター画面の印刷ボタンをクリックして、インクジェットのプリンターにデジタルのファイルを送ることに似ている。❷異なる点は、3Dプリンターはインクの代りに材料を連続する層状に堆積させていき、固体の物体を出現させることだ。❸その層は多くの方法で結合される。❹これらのうちの1つは、トレイの上に粉末を拡げて、それからレーザーや電子ビームで焼結し（熱を加えて）要求された形にそれを凝固させる。❺もう1つの方法は、溶解プラスチックのフィラメントを堆積させる。❻それぞれの層が完成した後、製作トレイをわずか1ミリ足らず下げて、次の層が加えられる。❼3Dプリントの大きな利点は、WYSIWYG（見た通りの物が手に入る）プロセスであることで、コンピューター画面上で作成する雛形とプリンターで作られた最終製品はほぼ同じである。

3 ❶10年以上の間、3Dプリンターは、製造業者が実物を生産するために工場に機械を備え付けるという費用のかかる業務を始める前に、素早く安く試作品を作る手段として使われてきた。❷しかし、このプリンターは急速に進化して、今や3Dプリンターの生産物の20%以上が最終製品を作るために使用されている。❸プリンター自体も迅速な印刷をするために開発されているが、今では複合押出ヘッドを使用し、印刷全体の速度を高めている機械もある。❹それぞれの複合ヘッド機は容易に再プログラム可能で、高付加価値の「顧客の要望に応える大量生産」の方法を切り開いている。

4 ❶3Dプリントが何よりも十分に発達していることを証明する一例は、飛行機の部品を作る際の使用である。❷3Dプリンターは現在、通常は金属の塊から作るチタンの着陸装置のブラケットを印刷するために使用されていて、製造業者は最終的に飛行機のエンジン全体をプリントすることを望んでいる。❸3Dプリンターがとくに航空機の製

造で重要になる可能性があるのは、軽量の部品を生産することに優れているからだ。❹小型機でさえ大量の高価なチタンを含む。❺これらの部品はたいてい金属片から機械加工され、結果として材料の90％が削りとられることもある。❻3Dプリントで同じ部品を作るためには、プリンターはトレイの上に約20-30ミクロン（0.02–0.03ミリ）の厚さにチタンの粉末を層状に拡げて、それからレーザーで結合させる。❼ほとんど廃棄の無駄がなく、その部品は目的に合わせて容易に最適化され、軽量だがたいていの場合は従来の工業部品と同じくらいの強度がある。❽このことが重要なのは、燃費のよい航空機を作るうえで軽さは決定的に重要だからだ。❾したがって、3D製造はより環境に優しい航空機を作ることに役立つ。

5 ❶3Dプリンターはコストとリスクを低減することで製造業を一変させる可能性もある。❷低コストなため生産者はもはや資本のもとを取るために数千もの品目を作る必要はなく、これによって従来は規模の経済でのみ克服された参入障壁が低減される。❸こうしたプリンターは「大量特注生産」の製造方法としても理想にかなっている。❹これは実際にすでに現実となっており、印刷サービスのなかには個人が自分のデザインをアップロードして、それを3Dプリンターで製造してもらうことを可能にしているところもある。

6 ❶3Dプリントの技術が改善されより主流になるにつれて、個人の要望に応じる部品作りの経済過程が劇的に変化し、まもなく「デジタル生産工場」の出現を見ることになるだろう。❷専用部品を必要とする企業は、地元でその部品をプリントしてもらったり自分たちでプリントしたりする方が他の国を拠点とする供給業者から注文するより、安くて速いと気づくかもしれない。❸製造業のなかには、中国などの安い生産拠点から西洋に戻ってくるところがあると推測されている。❹中国の会社もまた3Dプリント技術を採り入れているが、将来的には製品を輸送するコストのほうが地元で作る費用より上回るだろう。❺このことは、西洋の国々が自国に製造業を戻し始めるため、西洋の経済の押し上げを促すだろう。

7 ❶おそらく3Dプリントの最も素晴らしい側面は、工場を建てたり、大量生産業者に何か作ることを頼んだりする従来のルートより、より安くリスクの少ない市場へのルートを提供することだ。❷起業家はアイディアがうまくいくかどうかを確かめるために3Dプリンターでいくつかのサンプルを作ることができ、その製品が売れそうかどうかを確かめるためにサンプルをさらに数点作ることもできるだろう。❸もしその製品が成功すれば、そのビジネスは製造規模を拡大することができるだろう。❹その結果、製造業でのこれからの成功は、規模ではなくアイディアの質によるだろう。❺否定的側面は、良いアイディアが従来の製造工程よりもさらに速く3Dプリントでコピーされる可

能性があることだ。したがって、知的財産権をめぐる戦いが激化するかもしれない。

8 ❶来たるべき3Dプリントの普及は、将来に向けて他の不安を明らかにしている。❷2013年、テキサス大学法学部の学生コーディー・ウィルソンは人気の型のライフル銃のプラスチック製の30発装填可能な弾倉を製造するために、3Dプリンターをリースで期間借りし、それを首尾よく動作確認をした。❸このことは、新しい3Dプリント技術が危険な目的のために使うことが可能であるという不安につながった。❹アメリカ合衆国にはすでに一般的なX線機器で探知できない銃を禁止する法律があるが、もし技術が進み3Dプリンターを持つ人が自分の銃器を作ることができる状況になるなら、このようなプリント機器の法的な枠組みを再考することが必要かもしれない。

重要語句

☐ **deposit ...**	〔動〕…を堆積する、…を置く
☐ **subtractive**	〔形〕引き算の
☐ **prototype**	〔名〕型、試作品
☐ **a fraction of ...**	〔熟〕わずかな…
☐ **come of age**	〔熟〕成人に達する、十分に発達する
☐ **optimise ...**	〔動〕…を最適化する、…を最大限利用する
☐ **inference**	〔名〕推論、推理
☐ **boost ...**	〔動〕…を増大させる = increase
☐ **run off ...**	〔動〕…を複写する、…を刷る
☐ **ubiquity**	〔名〕遍在
☐ **throw up**	〔動〕もたらす、明らかにする

正解一覧

1 FALSE	**2** FALSE	**3** TRUE	**4** NOT GIVEN
5 TRUE	**6** C	**7** A	**8** F
9 D	**10** WYSIWYG	**11** economies of scale	
12 intellectual property rights		**13** firearms	

問題文和訳

Questions 1–5

以下の文は本文に与えられた情報と一致するか?
解答用紙の1–5の欄に…を書きなさい。

TRUE	もし文が情報と一致すれば
FALSE	もし文が情報に矛盾すれば
NOT GIVEN	もしこれについての情報がなければ

1   3Dプリントは新しい物体を作るのに減法工程に頼る。

2   3Dプリントが試作品を作るのに使用されたのはつい最近だ。

3   3Dプリントを使う1つの利点は、製造過程においてチタンの無駄がより少ないことだ。

4   3Dプリントの技術は他のどこよりも西洋で成功しそうだ。

5   起業家は現在進行中の3Dプリントの進化から恩恵を受けるだろう。

1   **|正解|** FALSE
1段落2文でsubtractive process（減法工程）がtraditional machining techniques（従来の機械加工技術）として言及されている。

2   **|正解|** FALSE
1段落3文で1970年代から試作品に使用されてきたとある。

3   **|正解|** TRUE
4段落5文、7文に相当。従来の方法では材料（チタン）が90％削られるが、3D印刷では殆ど材料の無駄がない。

4   **|正解|** NOT GIVEN
本文中に西洋で成功するだろうという具体的な記述はない。6段落3文は西洋での製造業の変化の可能性に言及している。

5   **|正解|** TRUE
7段落2-3文に企業が受けうる3Dプリントの恩恵についての記述がある。

▌問題文和訳

Questions 6–9
それぞれの文を、以下のA–Fから正しい文末を選んで完成しなさい。
解答用紙の6–9の欄にA–Fの正しいものを記入しなさい。

6   それぞれのプラスチックの層が熱を加えられた後、製作トレイは

7   3Dプリンターの生産の5分の1以上が

8   3Dプリントは航空機の生産に有用なのは、それが…だからだ

9   製造コストが下がるにつれ、企業は

第2章　解答解説

A	最終製品を製造するのに使われている
B	今やジェット機のエンジン全体を製造できる
C	下げられ、次の層に熱が加えられる
D	製造業を西洋に戻すことになるかもしれない
E	プログラミングの技術をもはや必要としない
F	軽量の部品を製造できる

6 正解 **C**

2段落6文がCに該当。

7 正解 **A**

3段落2文の内容及びプリンターの生産物の20％についての言及がAに該当。

8 正解 **F**

4段落3文にFに該当する言及あり。

9 正解 **D**

6段落終わりで同様の記述がある。

問題文和訳

Questions 10–13

以下の表を完成しなさい。

それぞれの解答を本文から3語以内で選び、解答用紙の10–13の欄に記入しなさい。

3Dプリントの利点と危険	
賛成	・頭文字**10** <u>WYSIWYG</u>が暗示するように、コンピューター画面で見るものを正確にプリントできる。 ・**11** <u>規模の経済</u>の必要性をなくすことによって、参入障壁を軽減させる。
反対	・デザインの複写の簡易化によって**12** <u>知的財産権</u>を巡る議論が増えることになるだろう。 ・セキュリティー上の現実の脅威は、人々が自分の**13** <u>銃器</u>を製造する危険性である。

10 |正解| WYSIWYG

2段落7文を参照。acronym（頭字語）の意味がわからなくても、設問文後半の内容で文中のどの部分を指しているか理解し、略語だと判断することが可能。

11 |正解| economies of scale

5段落2文で同様の記述がある。規模の経済と参入障壁の関係をおさえて解答する。

12 |正解| intellectual property rights

7段落5文で言及されている。文中のsoは問題文のresult inと同様と考える。

13 |正解| firearms

8段落4文後半に「3Dプリンターを持つ人が自分の銃器を作ることができる」とある。

第2章

解答解説

time: 20 minutes

You should spend about 20 minutes on **Questions 1–13,** which are based on the reading passage below.

Farm fish but not farm fresh

A   Aquaculture, in the form of fish farms, has proven extremely lucrative. It appeared at the right time to satisfy a growing demand for fish just as global stocks began to dwindle. According to some, however, this industry may be causing more harm than good. While it may be generating huge profits, many specialists warn that its impact on the marine ecosystem could prove disastrous in the long run.

B   A recent exposé highlighted a number of dangerous practices prevalent in the agro-food industry. One Norwegian environmentalist claimed that salmon farming was a disaster both for the environment and for human health. The operators of these farms stand accused of pumping tons of chemicals into the water to promote growth and protect against stock loss. Over time these chemicals settle, accumulate and mix with fish waste to form a thick deposit of bacteria, drugs and pesticides on the sea floor. Since the farms are located in open water, the pollution on the sea bed can easily spread and contaminate other areas.

C   A salmon farm can hold up to 2 million fish in a relatively small space. Crowded conditions such as these are conducive to the spread of disease. According to one expert, sea lice, Pancreas Disease and Infectious Salmon Anemia Virus are rampant in fish farms across Norway, yet consumers are never informed of outbreaks and the sale of diseased fish continues unabated. Indeed, the risk of such diseases prompts the use of even more dangerous pesticides, some of which are known to have neurotoxic effects. The pesticides used to keep sea lice in check can also affect the fish's DNA resulting in genetic mutations. Half of all farmed cod is said to be deformed and these mutations can easily spread to the wild population if a female cod escapes. Farm salmon also suffer mutation—their flesh is more "brittle" and readily breaks apart. In addition, the nutritional content is altered with a much higher fat content (15-35 per cent) compared with wild salmon (5-7 per cent fat). This is particularly alarming as toxins have been shown to accumulate most readily in fatty areas.

D   When compared to a number of different foods sold in Norway, farmed salmon was found to be five times more toxic than the other products tested. In animal studies, mice that were fed farmed salmon grew obese and formed thick layers of fat around their organs and developed diabetes. This raises a very worrying spectre for anyone who regularly consumes such fish.

E   Further investigation, however, reveals that the most significant source of toxins is not the pesticides or antibiotics administered to the farm fish but the dry pellet feed that forms their diet. Pollutants found in the pellets include dioxins, PCBs and a number of other drugs and chemicals. Pellets in at least one Norwegian plant were found to be made from eel, popular due to its high protein and fat content, and other fatty fish from the Baltic Sea.

F   A number of nations stand accused of allowing factories to dump industrial waste into the Baltic Sea. Once there, these toxins are absorbed by fish and bind to their fat cells. Species such as herring, eel and salmon are particularly vulnerable and can accumulate high levels of toxicity. As a result, fish mongers in Sweden are now required to warn patrons of the toxic levels of fish caught in Baltic waters. The government have issued guidelines recommending that consumers not eat fatty fish more than once a week and that anyone pregnant should avoid eating fish from the Baltic altogether.

G   Species that are deemed unfit for human consumption are thus used to produce fish pellets. And the process used to produce the pellets can further elevate their toxicity. Fish are cooked and broken down into two separate products: protein meal and oil. While the oil has high levels of dioxins and PCBs, an antioxidant called ethoxyquin is sometimes added to the protein powder. Ethoxyquin is a pesticide developed in the 1950's for use on fruits and vegetables. The fish feed industry, however, uses it to prevent fats from oxidising and going rancid and keeps this practice secret from the health authorities. Therefore, while the European Union regulates ethoxyquin levels in fruits, vegetables and meat, it does not do so for fish. Exploring this further, one Swiss laboratory was surprised to discover levels of ethoxyquin some 10 to 20 times higher than that allowed by the EU for other foods. This is all the more disconcerting as the effects of ethoxyquin on human health have yet to be established. The only research conducted to date was done by a Ph.D. student who found that ethoxyquin can cross the blood brain barrier and possibly have carcinogenic effects.

H It is clear that the health label once applied to fish needs to be reassessed. Fish farms do not offer a viable solution to the problems of overfishing, at least while the hazardous practices outlined above continue. Indeed, they may be making matters worse by harming the marine ecosystem that wild stocks depend on and creating more future health problems for those who consume them.

Questions 1–3

Answer the questions below.
*Choose **NO MORE THAN THREE WORDS** from the passage for the answer.*
Write your answers in boxes 1–3 on your answer sheet.

1 What biological network is at risk from current practices in aquaculture industry?

2   What is found to be changed among farm salmon?

3   What must Swedish merchants display when selling fish from the Baltic region?

Questions 4–8

Do the following statements reflect the claims of the writer in the reading passage?

In boxes 4–8 on your answer sheet, write

YES   *if the statement reflects the claims of the writer*

NO   *if the statement contradicts the claims of the writer*

NOT GIVEN   *if it is impossible to say what the writer thinks about this*

4   The agro-food industry has been financially unsuccessful.

5   The practices used in protecting farm fish carry an ecological cost.

6   Eating farm fish will cause obesity and diabetes among humans.

7   The health authorities colluded with the fish farm operators.

8   The European Union will implement stricter regulations in future.

Questions 9–13

The reading passage has eight paragraphs, **A–H**.

Which paragraph contains the following information?

*Write the correct letter, **A–H**, in boxes 9–13 on your answer sheet.*

9   criticism of an untested additive

10   irresponsible business practices of industrialised countries

11   the main factor contributing to toxicity among farmed fish

12   harmful impacts on farm fish

13   media revelations of harmful procedures

養殖魚は鮮魚ではない

A ❶養魚場という形態をとる水産養殖は非常に儲かるということが判明している。❷世界株式市場が縮小し始めたとき、高まる魚への需要を満たすためにちょうど良いタイミングで登場した。❸しかしながら、専門家によると、この産業は利益以上に害をもたらしている可能性がある。❹甚大な利益を生み出す一方で、海洋の生態系への影響が長期的に悲惨なものになりかねないと多くの専門家が警鐘を鳴らしている。

B ❶最近ある暴露記事が農業食品業界でいくつもの危険な慣習が蔓延していることを浮き彫りにした。❷あるノルウェーの環境保護主義者は、サケの養殖は環境的にも人体の健康にも悲惨であると言っている。❸こうした養殖場の経営者は、成長の促進や個体の損失を防ぐために水中に農薬を注入し続けていることから非難を受けている。❹長年に渡ってこうした化学物質が沈んで堆積し、魚の排泄物と混ざって海底にバクテリアや薬品や農薬の分厚い沈殿物を形成する。❺養殖場が開放水域にあるため、海底の汚染は簡単に広がり、他の場所も汚染する可能性がある。

C ❶サケの養殖場は、比較的小さなスペースに最大で200万匹の魚を入れることができる。❷こうした隙間のない環境では病気は広がりやすい。❸ある専門家によれば、フナムシや膵臓疾患やサケ感染症貧血ウイルスがノルウェー中の養魚場で蔓延しているが、消費者に病気の流行について知らされることがなく、病気に感染した魚の販売が減ることはない。❹実際のところ、こうした病気のリスクでさらに危険な殺虫剤や農薬の使用が促進されるが、なかには神経毒作用で知られているものもある。❺フナムシの繁殖の抑制に使われる殺虫剤は、魚のDNAに影響を及ぼし、遺伝子の突然変異をもたらす。❻養殖されたタラの半分は奇形だと言われていて、もしメスのタラが逃げ出してしまった場合にこうした変異が野生の個体群に簡単にひろがってしまう可能性がある。❼養殖されたサケも変異を受けていて、身の部分は普通のサケよりも「もろく」簡単にぼそぼそになる。❽さらに栄養素の含有量が変わり、天然のサケ（脂質5〜7%）と比較して脂質（15〜35%）の値がかなり高い。❾毒性が脂肪に最も簡単に蓄積することがわかっているため、このことは特に憂慮すべきことだ。

D ❶ノルウェーで販売されているたくさんの食品と比較したところ、養殖されたサケは検査された他の製品よりも毒性が5倍であることが判明した。❷動物実験では、養殖されたサケを与えられたマウスが肥満になり、臓器の周囲に厚い脂肪の層ができ、糖尿病を発症した。❸こうしたことは、このような魚をいつも消費する者にとって大きな不安の種である。

E ❶しかしながら、最も重大な毒素の出どころは養殖場で投与される殺虫剤でも抗生物質でもなく、餌となっている乾燥ペレットであることが、さらなる調査で明らかになった。❷ペレット中で検出された汚染物質には、ダイオキシン、PCB、そしてその他にも多くの化学薬品が含まれる。❸ノルウェーの少なくとも1つの工場で使われているペレットは、タンパク質と脂肪の含有量が高いことで需要のあるウナギや、バルト海産で獲れたその他の脂肪質の魚が原料であることわかった。

F ❶たくさんの国が、工場に産業廃棄物をバルト海に投棄させていることで非難されている。❷一旦海に廃棄されると、これらの毒は魚により吸収され体内の脂肪細胞と結合する。❸ニシン、ウナギ、サケのような種は特に影響を受けやすく、高濃度の毒を蓄積することがある。❹結果として、現在スウェーデンの魚屋には客にバルト海でとれた魚の毒性値を通知することが要求されている。❺スウェーデン政府は消費者に脂肪質の魚を1週間に1回以上食べないこと、妊婦はバルト海産の魚を完全に控えることを勧める指針を出している。

G ❶人間の消費に向かないとされる種の魚は、他の魚のペレットを製造するのに使われる。❷そして、そのペレットの製造過程がさらにその毒性を高めている。❸魚は調理され、タンパク質と油分の2つの生成物に分解される。❹油分は高濃度のダイオキシンとPCBを含む一方、エトキシキンと呼ばれる抗酸化物質が粉状のタンパク質に加えられる。❺エトキシキンは果物や野菜に使用するため1950年代に開発された殺虫剤である。❻しかし、養魚用飼料産業は、脂肪が酸化して油臭くなるのを防ぐために使用しているが、この慣習を保健機関に秘密にしている。❼したがって、EUはフルーツや野菜、肉に含まれるエトキシキンの濃度を規制しているが、魚には規制をしていない状況だ。❽この問題をさらに調査したところ、あるスイスの研究室はEUが他の食品に認めている約10倍から20倍以上も高いエトキシキン濃度であることを突き止めて驚愕した。❾エトキシキンの人間の健康への影響がまだ立証されていないため、このことは一層不安な事態だ。❿今までに行われた唯一の調査は博士課程の学生によるもので、エトキシキンには血液脳関門を通過し発がん効果の可能性があることを突き止めた。

H ❶かつて魚製品に取り付けられていた健康表示が見直される必要があることは明らかである。❷少なくとも先ほど概説された危険な慣習が続けられている間は、養魚場が過剰漁業の問題に対して実行可能な解決策を提示していることにはならない。❸実際のところ、養魚場は魚の野生種が依存している海洋生態系を害したり魚の消費者に将来的な健康問題をさらに引き起こしたりすることによって、事態を悪化させかねない。

重要語句

☐ **aquaculture**	〔名〕	魚介類の養殖
☐ **lucrative**	〔形〕	利益のあがる
☐ **dwindle**	〔動〕	（数量）が減少する、縮小する
☐ **highlight**	〔動〕	呼び物とする、目立たせる
☐ **deposit**	〔名〕	沈着
☐ **pancreas**	〔名〕	膵臓
☐ **unabated**	〔形〕	変わらない、減退しない
☐ **check**	〔名〕	抑制
☐ **toxin**	〔名〕	毒
☐ **diabetes**	〔名〕	糖尿病
☐ **antibiotic**	〔名〕	抗生物質
☐ **administer**	〔動〕	投与する
☐ **vulnerable**	〔形〕	（病気や危険などに）冒されやすい、無防備な
☐ **rancid**	〔形〕	油くさい
☐ **disconcerting**	〔形〕	当惑させるような
☐ **carcinogenic**	〔形〕	発がん性の
☐ **viable**	〔形〕	実行可能な

正解一覧

1 (the) marine ecosystem	**2** (the) nutritional content	
3 (the) toxic levels	**4** NO	**5** YES
6 NOT GIVEN	**7** NO	**8** NOT GIVEN	**9** G
10 F	**11** E	**12** C	**13** B

問題文和訳

Questions 1–3

以下の設問に答えなさい。

それぞれの解答を3語以内で本文から選びなさい。

解答用紙の1–3の欄に解答を記入しなさい。

1 養殖業の最近の行為によってどの生物学的ネットワークが危険にさらされているか。

2 養殖のサケには何の変化がみられるか。

3 スウェーデンの業者はバルト海地域からとれた魚を売るときに何を表示しなければならないか。

1 **正解** (the) marine ecosystem
A段落4文で海洋の生態系にもたらされる危険性について述べられている。

2 **正解** (the) nutritional content
C段落8文で栄養素の含有量の変化について述べられている。

3 **正解** (the) toxic levels
F段落4文目に毒性値の通知義務について述べられている。

問題文和訳

Questions 4–8

以下の文は本文の筆者の意見を反映しているか？

解答用紙の4–8の欄に以下のいずれかを記入しなさい。

YES	筆者の主張と一致している
NO	筆者の主張に矛盾する
NOT GIVEN	このことについての筆者の考えがわからない

4 農業食品業界は採算がとれていなかった。

5 養殖魚を保護するためになされる慣習は生態系を犠牲にする。

6 養殖魚を食べることは人間の肥満や糖尿病の原因となる。

7 保健機関は養魚場の経営者と共謀していた。

8 EUは将来的により厳しい規制を課す予定である。

4 |正解| **NO**

A段落1文に養魚場は儲かるビジネスであることが述べられている。

5 |正解| **YES**

A段落4文と段落Bで、魚の保護と引き換えに海洋生態系がダメージを受けていることについて述べられている。

6 |正解| **NOT GIVEN**

D段落でマウスの実験結果については述べられているが、人間の肥満や糖尿病と魚を食べることの因果関係についての情報はない。

7 |正解| **NO**

G段落から、保健機関は取り締まる側なので二者が共謀はしているわけではないことが読み取れる。

8 |正解| **NOT GIVEN**

EUによる将来的な規制については述べられていない。

> **問題文和訳**

Questions 9–13

本文にはA–Hの8段落がある。

以下の情報を含むのはどの段落か？

解答用紙の解答欄9–13にA–Hを記入しなさい。

9 検査を受けていない添加物への批判

10 産業国の無責任な商慣行

11 養殖魚の毒性をもたらす主な要因

12 養殖魚に対する悪影響

13 メディアによる有害な作業手順の暴露

9 |正解| **G**

G段落で、酸化防止として使用されているエトキシキンについて人体への影響にはまだ立証されていないが、発がん効果がある可能性が指摘されている。

10 |正解| **F**

F段落1文にたくさんの国による産業廃棄物の投棄について言及されている。

11 |正解| **E**

E段落1文に主な毒性の根源はペレットであると述べられている。

12 |正解| **C**

C段落で、養魚場での病気の蔓延と農薬や殺虫剤の使用について言及されている。

13 |正解| B

B段落１文で農業食品業界の危険な慣習が明らかになっと述べられている。

*You should spend about 20 minutes on **Questions 1–13**, which are based on the reading passage below.*

Out of Africa

The study of genetics has shown that the genetic variation among people in different parts of the world can serve as a map of humanity's expansion in prehistoric times. Now biologists have started applying the sophisticated statistics used in DNA studies to the study of historical linguistics. Dr Quentin Atkinson of the University of Auckland in New Zealand has counted the number of distinct sounds used in 504 languages around the world, and charted them on a map. The component of sound used was a 'phoneme', which is the smallest unit that allows us to distinguish one word from another, whether it is a vowel, consonant, or spoken tone. One example of a single phoneme difference would be that between the English words 'cat' and 'bat'. After counting the phonemes, Atkinson constructed a series of models to compare phonemic density in different populations.

Dr Atkinson found that the number of distinct sounds in a language tends to decrease as it gets farther away from sub-Saharan Africa, and he argues that these differences reflect the patterns of migration of our ancestors when they left the area 70,000 years ago. This discovery bore out his theory that if language arose in Africa, then the number of phonemes would be greatest in Africa and smallest in South America, which is the region farthest from Africa. The pattern that he found matches this prediction. The number of sounds does indeed vary greatly from language to language, and the variations are generally proportionate to distance.

Some of the African tribal languages have as many as 200 phonemes, while European languages contain far fewer. English, for example, has less than a quarter of this, and German slightly fewer than that. The languages of Asia, which is located geographically between Europe and America, tend to have around 30 phonemes. Asia's most widely spoken language, Mandarin, fits into this category. Finally, some South American languages have fewer than 15 phonemes. The Piraha language, spoken by the Amazonian tribe of the same name, comes at the farthest extreme with less than a dozen, two fewer than the outlier Hawaiian language.

Dr Atkinson's study was prompted by a recent finding that the number of phonemes in a language increases with the number of people who speak it. This led him to speculate that the diversity of phonemes would increase as a population grew, but would fall again when a small group split off and moved away from the parent group. The reduction in phonemic diversity over increasing distances from Africa, as seen by Dr Atkinson, parallels the reduction in genetic diversity already recorded by biologists. The continual 'budding' process, which is the means by which the first modern humans spread out across the world, is known to produce what biologists call a 'serial founder' effect—each time a smaller group moves away, its genetic diversity declines. For either genetic or phonemic diversity to reduce, the population budding process must be rapid, or diversity will build up again. The implication is that the human expansion out of Africa was very rapid at each stage. It is probable that this swift expansion became possible thanks to the human acquisition of modern languages.

Atkinson's model also indicates the migration and colonisation patterns of modern humans after they left the African heartland. Outside of Africa, the greatest phonemic diversity was found in languages thought to have arisen in Southeast Asia, which is consistent with the high levels of genetic diversity there. This suggests that Southeast Asian populations grew very rapidly soon after our first ancestors left Africa. Within the Americas, phonemic diversity diminished with distance from the Bering Strait (a narrow stretch of water that used to be a land bridge connecting Asia and what is now Alaska); that is to say, the phonemic diversity of a language group became smaller the farther away its population was located from the Bering Strait. This fits with assumptions that the first Americans used this land bridge to migrate from Asia before spreading south as far as the tip of South America.

Previous approaches to tracing the spread of languages had relied on changes in lexical or grammatical structures to build up a map of language evolution. Certain words have similar roots within a family of languages, though these roots have not been seen to extend across all languages. Thus in the Indo-European family, the Sanskrit word 'bhrater' is 'brathir' in Old Irish, 'frater' in Latin, 'phrater' in Greek, and 'brother' in English. To some extent these differences can be used to reconstruct the ancient words that gave rise to our modern ones. Unlike genes, however, it is difficult to investigate the origin of actual words beyond the era in which writing was invented. Dr Atkinson's approach opens up the possibility of extending language research even farther back into our prehistory.

Questions 1–4

*Choose the correct letter, **A**, **B**, **C** or **D**.*

Write your answers in boxes 1–4 on your answer sheet.

1   What did Dr Atkinson discover about phonemes?

   A   The word 'cat' and 'bat' share the same phonemes.

   B   The number of phonemes in a language decreases according to its distance from sub-Saharan Africa.

   C   South American languages tend to have greater phonemic density.

   D   Most of the world's languages use the same key phonemes.

2   How do the studies about phonemes and genetics relate to each other?

   A   They exhibit similar patterns of global distribution.

   B   They demonstrate that human expansion increases diversity.

   C   They confirm that diversity decreases over time.

   D   They show that phonemic density is a function of genetic variation.

3   What does the passage say about the Bering Strait?

   A   Long ago, it was narrower than it is today.

   B   It served as a land bridge for Americans to migrate to Asia.

   C   It is believed that the ancestors of South Americans crossed it.

   D   The number of sounds in a language increases farther from the Strait.

4   What was the main flaw with previous methods of studying language history?

   A   It was difficult to trace languages further than the beginnings of writing.

   B   They failed to identify sufficient lexical or grammatical structures.

   C   Researchers were unable to reconstruct the origin of modern words.

   D   There were too many language families with similar roots.

Questions 5–8

Look at the following map, and match the following languages with the number of phonemes for each language.

Write the correct letter, **A–F**, in boxes 5–8 on your answer sheet.

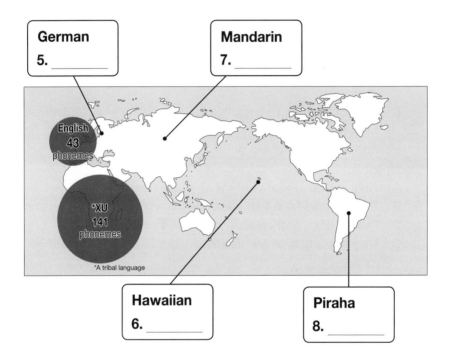

German
5. _____

Mandarin
7. _____

English
43
phonemes

°XU
141
phonemes

°A tribal language

Hawaiian
6. _____

Piraha
8. _____

A	200
B	13
C	41
D	32
E	8
F	11

Questions 9–13

Do the following statements agree with the information given in the reading passage?

In boxes 9–13 on your answer sheet, write

TRUE   *if the statement agrees with the information*
FALSE   *if the statement contradicts the information*
NOT GIVEN *if there is no information on this*

9   Dr Quentin Atkinson studied at the University of Auckland in New Zealand.
10   European languages generally have more phonemes than Asian languages.
11   A decrease in phonemic diversity depends on a rapid budding process.
12   The acquisition of modern languages halted the rate of human expansion.
13   The word for "brother" has a common root in all languages.

全文訳

アフリカから（アフリカ起源）

1 ❶遺伝学の研究は、世界の様々な地域の人々の遺伝的な多様性を有史以前の人類の拡散の地図としての役割を果たしうることを示している。❷生物学者は現在DNAの研究で使用される最新式の統計を歴史言語学の研究に適用し始めている。❸ニュージーランド、オークランド大学のクエンティーン・アトキンソン博士は、世界中の504の言語で使用されているはっきり区別できる音の数を数えて、地図を作成した。❹この際に使われた音の構成要素は「音素」であり、母音であっても子音であっても話されるときの音の抑揚であっても、1つの単語と他の単語の区別を可能にする音の最小単位である。❺単一の音素の違いの一例は、英単語の 'cat' と 'bat' の違いだろう。❻音素を数えた後、アトキンソンは様々な人間集団の音素の密度を比較するための一連のモデルを構築した。

2 ❶アトキンソン博士が発見したのは、1つの言語に固有な音の数はサハラ以南のアフリカから離れれば離れるほど減少する傾向があることだ。これらの違いは、7万年前に祖先がその地域を去った時の移住のパターンを反映しているのだと彼は主張している。❷この発見は、もしアフリカで言語が生まれたのであれば、音素の数はアフリカで最大で、アフリカから最も遠い地域である南米では最小になるという彼の説を裏付けた。❸彼が発見したパターンはこの予想に一致した。❹音の数は、実際に言語によって非常に異なり、その差異は一般的に距離に比例する。

3 ❶アフリカの部族言語の中には200もの音素があるものもある一方で、ヨーロッパの言語ははるかに少ない。❷例えば、英語はこの数の4分の1以下で、ドイツ語は英語より若干少ない。❸地理的にヨーロッパとアメリカの間に位置するアジアの言語は約30の音素を持つ傾向がある。❹アジアで最も普及している言語、マンダリン（標準中国語）はこのカテゴリーに当てはまる。❺最後に南米の言語の中には音素が15未満のものもある。❻ピラハー語は、同じ名前のアマゾンの部族に話されている言語だが、最少の12未満であり、離島のハワイ語よりも2つ少ない。

4 ❶アトキンソン博士の研究は、ある言語における音素の数はそれを話す人の数とともに増加するという最近の発見がきっかけだった。❷このことから彼は、人口が増えるにつれ、音素の多様性が増加するが、小集団が分岐して親集団から去ると再び減少するだろうと推測した。❸アトキンソン博士が考えた通り、アフリカからの距離が増すこと

に対する音素の多様性の減少は、生物学者によってすでに記録されていた遺伝的な多様性の減少と並行する。❹最初の現代人が世界中に広がった手段である断続的な「出芽」過程（＝拡散と発達）は、生物学者が「連続創始者」効果と呼ぶ物を生み出すことで知られており、小集団が移住して離れるたびにその遺伝的差異は減少する。❺遺伝的な多様性や音素の多様性が減少するには、人々の出芽過程は急速でなければならない。そうでなければ多様性が再び増すからだ。❻アフリカからの人類の拡散はそれぞれの段階で非常に急速だったことを暗示している。❼おそらく、このような急速な拡散は人類の現代言語の習得のおかげで可能だったのだろう。

5　❶アトキンソンのモデルは、現代人がアフリカの中心地を去った後の移住と定住のパターンも示している。❷アフリカの外では、音素の最大の多様性が東南アジアで生まれたと考えられる言語で見つかり、そこでの高い遺伝的多様性と一致している。❸これは私たちの最初の祖先がアフリカを去った後、すぐに東南アジアの人口が急速に増えたことを示している。❹南北アメリカ大陸では、音素の多様性はベーリング海峡（アジアと現在のアラスカをつなぐ、昔陸の橋だった長く伸びる海域）からの距離とともに縮小した。つまり、人口分布の位置がベーリング海峡から離れれば離れるほど、言語集団の音素の多様性が減少したということだ。❺これは最初のアメリカ人が、南アメリカの先端まで南下して拡がる前にこの陸の橋を使ってアジアから移住したという仮定と一致する。

6　❶言語の広がりを追跡するこれまでの取り組み方は、言語の進化の地図を作成するのに語彙や文法の構造の変化に頼っていた。❷単語のなかには1つの語族の中に似たようなルーツを持つものもあるが、これらのルーツが全ての言語に広がることは見出されていない。❸ゆえにインド・ヨーロッパ語族では、サンスクリット語の 'bhrater' は古アイルランド語の 'brathir'、ラテン語の 'frater'、ギリシャ語の 'phrater'、英語の 'brother' に相当する。❹ある程度は、このような違いを利用して現代語の単語を生み出した古代の単語を再構築することができる。❺しかし遺伝子と違って、文字が発明された時代を超えて実際の単語の起源を調べることは難しい。❻アトキンソン博士の取り組みは私達の有史以前よりはるかに遡って言語の研究を拡げる可能性を切り開いている。

重要語句

- □ **sophisticated**　〔形〕洗練された、複雑な
- □ **bear out…**　〔動〕…を実証する、…を裏付ける
- □ **proportionate to ...**　〔形〕…に比例する
- □ **as many as ＋ 数詞**　〔熟〕（数ほど）も
- □ **speculate that ...**　〔動〕…だと推測する、考察する

□ build up	〔動〕高まる、増大する
□ consistent with ...	〔形〕…と一致する
□ diminish	〔動〕…を減らす
□ to some extent	〔熟〕ある程度
□ give rise to ...	〔熟〕…を生む

正解一覧

1 B	**2** A	**3** C	**4** A	**5** C	**6** B
7 D	**8** F	**9** NOT GIVEN		**10** TRUE	
11 TRUE		**12** FALSE		**13** FALSE	

問題文和訳

Questions 1–4

正しいものをA, B, C, Dから選びなさい。解答用紙の1–4の欄に解答を記入しなさい。

1 アトキンソン博士は音素について何を発見したか？

A 'cat'と'bat'は同じ音素を共有している。

B 言語における音素の数はサハラ以南のアフリカからの距離とともにその数が減少する。

C 南米の言語は非常に多くの音素を持つ傾向がある。

D 世界の言語の大半は同じ重要な音素を使っている。

2 音素と遺伝学の研究は互いにどのように関連するのか？

A それらは同じパターンの世界的分布を示す。

B それらは人類の拡散が多様性を増加させることを示す。

C それらは時間と共に多様性が減少する裏付けとなる。

D それらは音素の密度が遺伝的多様性の働きであることを示す。

3 ベーリング海峡について本文はどのように述べているか？

A ずっと昔、海峡の幅は今日よりもっと狭かった。

B アメリカ人がアジアに移住する陸の橋の役割を果たした。

C 南アメリカ人の祖先がそれを渡ったと考えられている。

D 言語における音の数は海峡から離れるほど増加する。

4 言語の歴史を研究するための以前の方法の主な欠点は何だったか？

A 文字の始まり以前の言語を追跡することが難しかった。

B それらは語彙的、文法的構造を特定できなかった。

C 研究者が現代語の単語の起源を再構築できなかった。

D 似たような起源をもつ言語族があまりにも多かった。

1 |正解| B

2段落1文にアトキンソン博士が発見した内容の言及がありBと一致する。Aは音素の具体例であり、3段落4文の記述はCと内容が逆である。Dに相当する記述はない。

2 |正解| A

4段落3文に「音素的の多様性と遺伝的多様性は並行する」という趣旨の記述がある。

3 |正解| C

ベーリング海峡については5段4文括弧内で「昔は陸の橋だった」とあり、5段落最終文で「この陸の橋を使ってアジアから移住したという仮定と一致」とあるのでCが正解。

4 |正解| A

最終段落5文「文字のない時代の言葉の起源を調べることは難しい」という趣旨の記述があるのでAに一致。6文で「アトキンソン博士の研究が有史以前の言語の調査の可能性を開く」という記述もある。

Questions 5–8

以下の地図を見て、それぞれの言語の音素の数と以下の言語を一致させなさい。
解答用紙の5–8の欄に正しいA–Fを記入しなさい。

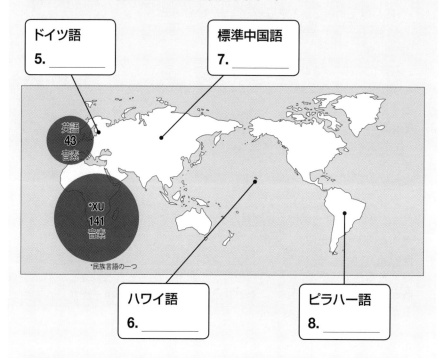

A	200
B	13
C	41
D	32
E	8
F	11

5　正解　C
6　正解　B
7　正解　D
8　正解　F

3段落1文に「アフリカの部族言語の中には200もの音素があるものもある」とあるので、Aは4つの言語のどれとも一致しない。3段落2文以降でドイツ語は英語よりもやや少なく、アジアの言語は約30と説明している。ピラハー語については3段落最後の... less than a dozen, two fewer than the outlier Hawaiian languageという記述から11で、ハワイ語は13だとわかる。

問題文和訳

Questions 9–13

以下の文章は本文の情報と一致するか？
解答用紙の9–13の欄に…を記入しなさい。

TRUE　　　　文章が情報と一致していれば
FALSE　　　　文章が情報と矛盾していれば
NOT GIVEN　　これに関する情報がなければ

9　　アトキンソン博士はニュージーランドのオークランド大学で学んだ。
10　ヨーロッパの言語は一般的にアジアの言語より音素が多い。
11　音素の多様性の減少は急激な発芽過程による。
12　現代語の習得が人類の拡散の速度を停止した。
13　"brother"を意味する単語はすべての言語に共通のルーツがある。

9　|正解|　NOT GIVEN
1段落3文に「ニュージーランド、オークランド大学のクエンティーン・アトキンソン博士」とあるが、アトキンソンがオークランド大学で学んだかどうかについての記述はない。

10　|正解|　TRUE
3段落の内容と一致する。

11　|正解|　TRUE
4段落5文for以下で、多様性が減少するのは集団が分岐する出芽過程が急速なためだとある。

12　|正解|　FALSE
4段落7文によれば、言語の習得は急速な拡散を抑制したのではなく促進した。

13　|正解|　FALSE
6段落2文後半に「一つの語体系の中に見られるが、様々な言語を超えて見ることはない」とあるのですべての言語の中ではない。

You should spend about 20 minutes on **Questions 1–13,** *which are based on the reading passage below.*

A Question of Life and Death

Interest in the study of moral philosophy as a way to help clarify problems and point the way to solutions is growing fast. Hitherto, moral philosophy was considered a rarefied branch of thinking that had little to do with the real world, but recently it has become a popular subject thanks to figures such as Michael Sandel, a professor at Harvard University whose lecture series '*Justice*' has been a huge hit on YouTube. Now moral philosophy is increasingly being applied to real-life situations, especially in the area of medicine, where the right and wrong choices are not always clear-cut. Moral philosophy helps us make tough choices about whether to prioritise, for example, a cheap medicine which offers minor benefits to many people or an expensive one which offers significant benefits to only a few. When considering these dilemmas, moral philosophers draw on the help of historical philosophers. The following problem demonstrates how moral philosophy can help in real-world cases.

Sam's wife is dying from a rare illness, but doctors believe there is one drug that might save her if she takes it for several months. The problem is that the drug is very expensive, and the woman's husband can only afford to buy enough to last for two weeks. He tries to get a loan from the bank, without success, and then tries to raise funds from among his friends, again without success. In desperation, he breaks into a pharmacy that sells the drug and steals enough pills to last for six months. He takes nothing else. Did he do the right thing? While most people might agree with what Sam did, many would also say that stealing is wrong. How can this paradox be resolved? The philosophical greats Kant, Mill, and Aristotle can provide us with insights into this issue.

Immanuel Kant (1724–1804) believed that we should use universal rules, or 'maxims', such as always telling the truth, to guide us when making decisions, and that we should follow these rules at all times. Since the consequences of an action are difficult to predict, we should not try to figure them out, but ignore them in deference to our maxims.

Aristotle (384–322 BCE) believed that anything which helps us develop as people is desirable, while anything that limits our growth is best avoided. Aristotle emphasised the social aspects of human development including family ties and education. He held that you should base your actions on your image of who you want to become and that you would grow to become that person through the repetition of actions consistent with that self-image.

John Stuart Mill (1806–1873) believed in the moral principle of 'the greatest happiness of the greatest number', initially expressed by Jeremy Bentham. Mill held that any attempt to act morally must first consider the consequences of an action. Behaviour tends to be good or bad depending on how useful it is—in other words, on its 'utility'. This principle became known as 'utilitarianism'.

In the scenario we are considering here, Kant would be against the decision to steal. He believed that we had to live by universal rules, and not stealing is one of them. One possible consequence of stealing, of course, is that Sam's wife could get better, but another is that Sam could be caught by the police and spend time in prison. Since we can never predict all the results of our actions, we do not need to consider them. Therefore, Kant would be quick to pronounce Sam's actions as wrong.

Aristotle would agree with Kant. He would say that you should act according to your image of the person you want to become. On that basis, Sam should refrain from stealing—unless, of course, he has ambitions to become a thief! Moreover, Aristotle valued the elements that are necessary for people to develop within a society. A society where stealing is common would not be a virtuous one.

Mill, on the other hand, would say that Sam would be acting morally if his actions brought happiness to the greatest number of people. In the case we are dealing with here, Sam's actions are likely to benefit Sam and his wife, but set against this is the loss of the potential profit the pharmaceutical company would have made from the sale of the drug. On balance, it would be fair to surmise that the benefit resulting from Sam's action would outweigh the loss to the pharmaceutical company of one set of pills. In this case, therefore, Mill would be likely to support Sam's decision. But what if Sam's actions were emulated by others? This is where the philosophical waters start to get muddied.

Questions 1–4

*Choose the correct letter, **A**, **B**, **C** or **D**.*
Write your answers in boxes 1–4 on your answer sheet.

1   What is Michael Sandel well known for?
   A   Producing a TV series called 'Justice'
   B   Making tough choices in real-life situations
   C   Lecturing at Harvard University
   D   Popularising moral philosophy

2   On hearing about his wife's illness, Sam's first action was to
   A   break into a pharmacy and steal pills.
   B   borrow money from his friends.
   C   request a loan from the bank.
   D   buy two weeks supply of the drug.

3   What dilemma is discussed in the passage?
   A   While legally wrong, many people would do what Sam did.
   B   Philosophers disagree about what Sam should have done.
   C   The actions of one can harm the majority.
   D   The rights of the many outweigh those of the individual.

4   Which philosophers would advise against Sam's actions?
   A   Kant, Aristotle, and Mill
   B   Kant and Aristotle
   C   Kant and Mill
   D   Aristotle and Mill

Questions 5–7

*Look at the following philosophers and the list of descriptions below. Choose one letter, **A, B, C** or **D**, to match the description of each philosopher below.*

*Write the correct letter, **A, B, C** or **D**, in boxes 5–7 on your answer sheet.*

5   Immanuel Kant

6   Aristotle

7   John Stuart Mill

A   We should consider our actions in light of our ideal self-image. As such thievery would only be appropriate for those pursuing a career in crime.

B   Due to the unpredictable consequences of any action we take it is best to stick to established axioms.

C   We should reject the idea that illegal actions can have a greater benefit than their cost.

D   To decide if Sam's actions are acceptable they must be weighed against the loss experienced by the corporation.

Complete the summary.

*Choose **NO MORE THAN TWO WORDS** from the passage for each answer.*

Write your answers in boxes 8–13 on your answer sheet.

In the past, **8** _____ was seen as a **9** _____ area of knowledge, but recently it has become popular as a way to help make difficult choices. To look into moral **10** _____ the reader has to decide whether Sam did the right thing in stealing a drug that would help prevent his wife's illness, enlisting the help of three philosophers. These thinkers were Kant, who recommended sticking to moral rules of guidance, or **11** _____; Aristotle, who believed anything that helped us grow as people was good; and Mill, who wanted to maximise **12** _____ with a philosophy known as **13** _____. An analysis of the philosophers' ideas reveals different viewpoints to guide us to our conclusion.

第2章

Exercise

NO TEST MATERIAL ON THIS PAGE

Exercise 10 解答解説

全文訳

生死の問題

1 ❶問題を明確にして解決法を示すのに役立つ方法としての道徳哲学への関心が急速に高まっている。❷これまで道徳哲学は実世界にほとんど関係のない高尚な思考の分野だと考えられていたが、講義シリーズ『Justice』*がYouTubeで大ヒットした、ハーバード大学のマイケル・サンデル教授のような人物のおかげで、近年人気の学科になった。❸現在道徳哲学は実生活の場面、とりわけ正しい選択と間違った選択が常にはっきりとしているわけではない医療分野でますます適用されてきている。❹道徳哲学はどちらを優先するのか難しい選択をするのに役に立つ。例えば、多くの人々にあまり有効でない安い薬を処方するのか、ほんのわずかな人々にだけ大いに効果がある高額なものを処方するのかといった選択である。❺こうしたジレンマを考える時、道徳哲学者は歴史上の哲学者をたのみとする。❻以下の問題はどのように道徳哲学が実世界のケースで役立つかを表している。

2 ❶サムの妻が稀な病で死にかけていたが、医師達はある薬を数カ月服用すれば彼女を救えるかもしれないと思っていた。❷問題はその薬が高価で、夫は二週間分を購入する程度の余裕しかないことだ。❸彼は銀行からローンを組もうとしたが成功せず、友人の間で資金を集めようとしたが、またも成功しなかった。❹やけになってその薬を販売している薬局に侵入し、6カ月は服用するのに十分な量の薬を盗んだ。❺彼は他に何も盗まなかった。❻彼は正しいことをしたのだろうか？❼ほとんどの人はサムがしたことに同情するかもしれないが、多くの人は盗みは悪いことだとも言うだろう。❽この矛盾はどのように解決できるだろうか。❾哲学の大家カント、ミル、アリストテレスは、この問題を理解する手がかりを私たちに与えてくれる。

3 ❶イマニュエル・カント（1724–1804）は、決断を下す時に私たちを導いてくれるような、常に真実を示すような普遍的規則、すなわち「格律」を用いるべきであり、私たちは常にこの規則に従うべきだと信じた。❷行動の結果は予測が難しいので、私たちはそれらを導き出そうとすべきでなく、結果は無視して格律に従うべきである。

4 ❶アリストテレス（西暦紀元前384–322）は、なんであれ私たちを人間として成長させるものは望ましいと信じた。一方で、成長を制限するものは避けるのが良いとも考えていた。❷アリストテレスは家族の絆と教育を含む人間の成長の社会的側面を強調し

174

た。❸ 彼は、人はこうなりたいと望む自己イメージを基に行動すべきだと考え、そして自己イメージと一致する行動を繰り返すことで思い描いた人間になれると考えた。

5 ❶ ジョン・ステュアート・ミル（1806–1873）は、元々はジェレミ・ベンサムにより唱えられた「最大多数の最大幸福」という道徳原則を信じていた。❷ ミルは、いかなる道徳的行為の試みであっても最初に行動の結果を検討しなければならないと主張した。❸ ふるまいの善し悪しはその有効性にある、言い換えればその「功利」による。❹ この原則は「功利主義」として知られている。

6 ❶ 私たちがここで考察しているシナリオでは、カントは盗むという決断に反対だろう。❷ 彼は普遍的ルールに従って生きるべきだと信じていて、盗みを働かない事はそうしたルールの一つである。❸ 盗んだ結果、もちろんサムの妻は回復する可能性もあるが、サムは警察につかまり刑務所で過ごす可能性もある。❹ 私たちは自分たちの行動の結果を全て予測することはできないので、結果について考える必要はない。❺ ゆえに、カントはサムの行動はまちがっているとすぐに宣言するだろう。

7 ❶ アリストテレスはカントと意見が一致するだろう。❷ 彼は自分がなりたいか望む人物のイメージに従って行動すべきだと言っている。❸ これを根拠に、サムは盗むことをやめるべきだ。もちろん、彼が泥棒になりたいという野望を持っていない場合の話だが！❹ さらに、アリストテレスは社会の中で人々が成長するのに必要な要素を尊重した。❺ 盗みが一般的な社会は高潔な社会ではないだろう。

8 ❶ 他方で、もしサムの行動が最大数の人々に幸福をもたらすのであれば、彼は道徳的に行動しているのだとミルは言うだろう。❷ 我々がここで扱っているケースの場合、サムの行動はサムと妻のためになりそうだが、これに対するのは、製薬会社が薬の販売から得たであろう潜在的な利益の損失である。❸ 結局、サムの行動から結果的に生じた利益が製薬会社の被る錠剤一式分の損失を上回ると推測するのが妥当だろう。❹ 従って、この場合、ミルはサムの決断を支持するだろう。❺ しかし、もしサムの行動が他の人に真似られたらどうだろうか。❻ この点において、哲学の問題はややこしくなる。

* 『Justice』：邦題 『ハーバード白熱教室』 早川書房

重要語句

☐ **clarify ...**	〔動〕…を明らかにする
☐ **have little to do with ...**	〔熟〕…とほとんど関係がない
☐ **draw on ...**	〔動〕…を利用する、あてにする

□ **maxim**	〔名〕格律、行動原理、格律 ＝ principle《カントの哲学用語としては格律》
□ **in deference to ...**	〔熟〕…に従って
□ **virtuous**	〔形〕高潔な
□ **in terms of ...**	〔熟〕…の点から
□ **according to ...**	〔熟〕(計画、規則などに) 従って《文中の時》
□ **refrain from ...**	〔熟〕…を差し控える
□ **surmise that ...**	〔動〕…だと推測する

正解一覧

1 D	**2** C	**3** A	**4** B	**5** B	**6** A	**7** D

8 moral philosophy   **9** rarefied   **10** dilemmas

11 maxims   **12** happiness   **13** utilitarianism

問題文和訳

Questions 1–4

正しいものをA, B, C, Dから選びなさい。解答用紙の1–4の欄に解答を記入しなさい。

1 マイケル・サンデルは何で有名か。
- **A** 'Justice'というテレビ・シリーズをプロデュースしたこと
- **B** 実生活で難しい選択をしたこと
- **C** ハーバード大学で講義をしていること
- **D** 道徳哲学を社会に広めたこと

2 妻の病気を知って、サムが最初に取った行動は…
- **A** 薬局に押し入り薬を盗んだこと
- **B** 友人から金を借りたこと
- **C** 銀行にローンを申請したこと
- **D** 2週間分の薬を買ったこと

3 本文ではどんなジレンマが論じられているか。
- **A** 違法だが、多くの人はサムがしたことをするだろう。
- **B** サムが何をすべきだったのか、哲学者達の間で意見が異なる。

C　一人の行動が大多数に害を及ぼしうる。

D　多数の権利が個人のそれにまさる。

4　どの哲学者がサムの行動と反対の忠告をするだろうか。

A　カント、アリストテレスとミル

B　カントとアリストテレス

C　カントとミル

D　アリストテレスとミル

1　|正解|　**D**

1段落2文に「道徳哲学が彼のおかげで人気の学科になった」とあるのでDが正解となる。

2　|正解|　**C**

2段落3文に「銀行からローンを借りようとした」とあるのでCが正解。その後、友人から資金集めをしようとしてうまくいかず、最後は薬局に盗みに入った。

3　|正解|　**A**

ジレンマの具体例を説明しているのはAである。Bは間違った内容ではないが、ジレンマの説明になっていない。CとDについては、大多数の害や個人の権利に関する具体的な記述がない。

4　|正解|　**B**

6段落1文で「カントは盗みの決断に反対だろう」とあり、7段落1文で「アリストテレスはカントと意見が一致するだろう」と言及。8段落1文で「ミルはサムが道徳的行為をしたと言うだろう」と肯定しているので、反対はカントとアリストテレスになる。

問題文和訳

Questions 5–7

以下の哲学者と説明文のリストを見なさい。

下のそれぞれの哲学者の説明と一致するものをA–Cから選び、解答用紙の5–7の欄に正しいものを記入しなさい。

5　イマニュエル・カント

6　アリストテレス

7　ジョン・ステュワート・ミル

A 私達は理想的な自己イメージを踏まえて自分の行動を検討すべきだ。窃盗行為そのものは犯罪でキャリアを積みたい者にだけ適正だろう。

B いかなる行動も推測不可能なため、確立された原則に遵守するのが最善である。

C 違法行為が代償以上に大きな恩恵をもたらしうるという考えは拒絶すべきだ。

D サムの行動が許容できるかどうか判断するには、彼の行動と企業の損失を天秤にかけなくてはならない。

5 正解 **B**
カントの考えについては3段落2文で格律に従うべきとあり、6段落2文で「普遍的なルールに従って生きるべきだ」と再度言及されている。

6 正解 **A**
アリストテレスについては4段落3文で「なりたい自分をイメージして、自己イメージを貫いて行動する」という趣旨の主張が述べられている。

7 正解 **D**
8段落3文でサムの行動と製薬会社の損失と比較検討するという結論が示されている。

問題文和訳

Questions 8–13
要約を完成しなさい。
それぞれの解答として、本文から2語以内の言葉を選び、解答用紙の8–13の欄に記入しなさい。

以前、**8** 道徳哲学 は **9** 高尚な 学問分野と見なされていたが、最近は難しい選択をするのに役立つ方法として普及している。道徳的な **10** ジレンマ について考察するため、サムは妻の病気を食い止めるのに役立つ薬を盗んだ際に正しいことをしたかどうかを、3人の哲学者の助けを得ながら、読者は判断しなければならない。その思想家とは、指針としての道徳的規則、すなわち **11** 格律 に固執することを推奨するカント；人間として私達が成長するのに役立つことはどんなことでも良いと信じたアリストテレス；そして **13** 功利主義 として知られる哲学で **12** 幸福 を最大化することを望んだミルの3人だ。哲学者の思想の分析は私達を結論に導く様々な視点を明らかにしている。

8 |正解| moral philosophy
1段落2文で言及。

9 |正解| rarefied
1段落2文で言及。

10 |正解| dilemmas
1段落5文 these dilemmas の記述から6文の The following problem ... となる2段落のサムの例に続いている。

11 |正解| maxims
3段落にカントの助言があり、1文に maxims の言及がある。

12 |正解| happiness
5段落2文で言及。

13 |正解| utilitarianism
5段落1文に「最大多数の最大幸福」、2文に「功利主義」の言及がある。

第2章

解答解説

*You should spend about 20 minutes on **Questions 1–13,** which are based on the reading passage below.*

Keynes vs Hayek: The Economic Fight of the Century

A   Every discipline has its greats. The ideas of Albert Einstein still reverberate in scientific thinking today, and Picasso had a huge influence on 20th century art. The discipline of economics is doubly blessed in that it has not one giant, but two—John Maynard Keynes and Friedrich August Hayek. Both were active in the Great Depression era, and the argument they had in the 1930s is one of the most famous in the history of economic thought. Their ideas are still significant in the economic policies of today.

B   The Great Depression was a period of severe economic downturn that affected much of the world in the decade leading up to World War II. It was the longest and deepest downturn of the 20th century. The depression originated in the United States and had a major impact on personal income, taxes, profits, and prices. During this time, industrial production plunged while unemployment reached 25% in the U.S. and even higher in some other countries.

C   Keynes (1883–1946) was an English economist whose ideas are said to have helped the U.S. pull itself out of recession. His prescription to recover from the deficit was for the government to spend its way out. He thought that governments should engage in deficit spending during depressions in order to increase the total level of demand for goods and services, known as aggregate demand. He believed economies are driven by consumption as opposed to production, and that money needed to be pumped into a circular flow in order to help the economy recover.

D   Hayek (1899–1992) was an Austrian economist (though he later became a British citizen) who opposed the Keynesian model of economics. He was a free-market, laissez-faire thinker who saw the economy not as a government-dominated enterprise but as a collection of individuals engaging in production and trade. From Hayek's perspective, the economy is driven by production, not consumption, and spending by the government, especially deficit spending, just upsets the natural economic balance. He promoted the idea that private investment would promote sustainable growth.

E   In 1936 Keynes published his "General Theory of Employment, Money, and Interest", now recognised as his magnum opus, to explain why the recovery from the Great Depression had been so weak. He thought that there was no automatic force for recovery in a market economy following a big shock, such as a collapse in investment, and that the economy would keep shrinking until it reached stability at a lower level, which he called 'underemployment equilibrium'. The reason was that the level of activity depended on demand, or spending power, and if that shrank, output would shrink too, creating a vicious cycle. In this situation, it was the government's job to increase its own spending in order to reverse the decline in consumer spending. The government could take up this role by running a deficit, and the money spent would spread throughout the economy through a multiplier effect, creating a virtuous cycle.

F   Hayek gave a different explanation. He claimed that the Keynesian model just produces a series of booms and busts. The booms begin when the government or banks expand credit or reduce interest rates to artificially lower levels, which encourages people to take out cheap loans. After a while, interest rates return to market levels, and then people realise that they cannot afford all of the credit that they have accrued. They stop spending, production goes down, and a bust soon follows.

G   To Hayek's mind, when a government engages in deficit spending, it only makes things worse. Hayek felt that banks and companies had to be made aware of the consequences of failure. If a government

第2章 Exercise

steps in to help banks and companies that are considered 'too big to fail', they are essentially spared the consequences of their actions, and so they are likely to repeat the same mistakes and keep coming back for more handouts. Supporters of Hayek stress that there is no painless recovery from an unsustainable boom that turns to bust. The only way to have no pain is to avoid the boom itself.

H Since Keynes believed in government action during times of financial crisis, it is often thought that Hayek believed in doing nothing, but this is wrong. He felt government had a lot to do in order to aid recovery in terms of deregulating business to stimulate innovation and growth, and in lightening the tax burden so that families and businesses would have more money to spend and invest.

I People were more attracted to Keynes' ideas of public spending than they were to Hayek's more austere approach, and Keynes' ideas were the ones adopted during the Depression era. Keynes is popularly credited with helping to end the Depression by providing the theory behind President Roosevelt's New Deal. It was not until some years after World War II that people began to pay serious attention to Hayek, but once they did Hayek's ideas gained ascendancy. Hayek won the Nobel Prize for Economics in 1974, and his ideas were put into practice in the U.S. monetarist policies of the 1980s.

Questions 1–6

*The reading passage has nine paragraphs, **A–I**.*
Which paragraph contains the following information?
*Write the correct letter, **A–I**, in boxes 1–6 on your answer sheet.*

1 Keynes' ideas were naturally more appealing than those of Hayek.
2 It is the government's responsibility to spend in order to counter a depression.
3 It is important to let an overspending bank fail so that banks can learn.

4   The Great Depression lasted for about ten years.

5   Hayek preferred to see private investment to government spending.

6   Hayek felt the government had a responsibility to reduce taxes.

Questions 7–10

Label the diagrams below.

*Choose **NO MORE THAN THREE WORDS** from the passage for each answer.*

Write your answers in boxes 7–10 on your answer sheet.

Keynes' theory

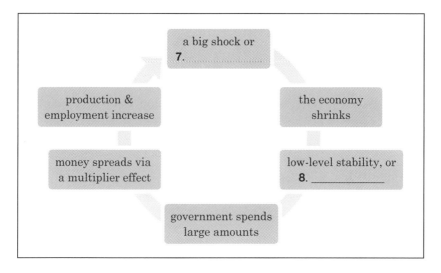

Hayek's theory

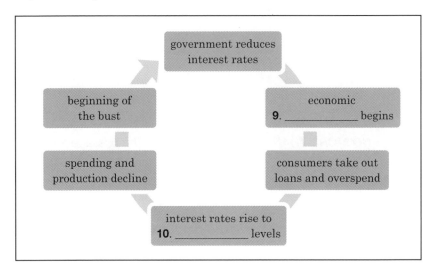

Questions 11–13

Do the following statements agree with the information given in the reading passage?

In boxes 11–13 on your answer sheet, write

TRUE   *if the statement agrees with the information*
FALSE   *if the statement contradicts the information*
NOT GIVEN *if there is no information on this*

11 Keynes felt that an economy would not automatically recover from a downturn.
12 Keynes believed that the government's role was to restrain spending in economically hard times.
13 Hayek felt that the banking system should be completely restructured.

第2章

Exercise

NO TEST MATERIAL ON THIS PAGE

Exercise 11　解答解説

全文訳

ケインズ対ハイエク：世紀の経済の論争

A ❶あらゆる学問分野には偉人がいる。❷アルバート・アインシュタインの考えは今日でも広く科学思想に影響を及ぼし、ピカソは20世紀の芸術に多大な影響を与えた。❸経済学の分野は1人の偉人ではなく、ジョン・メイナード・ケインズとフリードリッヒ・オーガスト・ハイエクの2人がいるという点で二重に恵まれている。❹両者とも大恐慌の時代に活躍し、1930年代に彼らが行った論争は、経済思想の歴史上で最も有名なものの1つだ。❺彼らの思想はいまだに今日の経済政策において重要である。

B ❶大恐慌は、第二次世界大戦に至る10年間で世界の大部分に影響をもたらした厳しい景気低迷の期間だった。❷それは20世紀で最も長く最も大きな下落だった。❸不況はアメリカ合衆国で始まり、個人収入、税金、利益率、物価に大きな影響を与えた。❹この間工業生産高が激減したが、アメリカでは失業率が25％に達し、他の国々でさらに高い所もあった。

C ❶ケインズ（1883–1946）は英国人の経済学者で、その理論はアメリカ合州国が不況から抜け出すのに役立ったといわれる。❷赤字から回復するための彼の処方箋は、政府が支出して切り抜けることだった。❸総需要として知られる品物とサービスの全体的な需要水準を引き上げるために、不況の間は政府が赤字財政支出に従事するべきだと彼は考えた。❹経済は生産と対にある消費で牽引され、経済の回復を促進するためには、貨幣を循環的流れの中に注入する必要があると彼は信じた。

D ❶ハイエク（1899–1992）はオーストリア人の経済学者で（後に英国国民になったが）ケインズ派経済理論に反対していた。❷彼は自由市場、自由放任主義の思想家で、経済を政府主導の事業ではなく、生産と商売に従事する個人の集まりと見なした。❸ハイエクの観点から見ると、経済は消費によってではなく生産によって動かされ、政府による支出、特に赤字財政支出は本来の経済の均衡を乱すだけだ。❹彼は民間の投資が持続可能な成長を促進するのだという考えを推奨した。

E ❶1936年、ケインズは彼の「雇用、利子、および貨幣の一般理論」を発表したが、現在、大恐慌からの回復力がこれほど弱かった理由を説明する彼の代表作として見

なされている。❷投資の破綻のような大きな衝撃の後に市場経済には自然発生的な回復力がなく、ケインズが「不完全雇用均衡」と呼んだ低レベルの安定に達するまで経済は縮小し続けると彼は考えた。❸その理由は、活動水準が需要や購買力に依存しており、もしこれが収縮すれば生産高も収縮し、悪循環を生みだすことになるからだ。❹このような状況で、消費者支出の下落を逆転するために支出を増やすことが政府の仕事だった。❺政府なら赤字経営によってこの役割を果たすことが可能で、消費された金が乗数効果で経済全体に広がり、好循環を生み出すというものだった。

F　❶ハイエクはこれとは異なる説明をした。❷ケインズ派理論は一連の好況と不況を生み出しているだけだと主張した。❸政府や銀行が貸付金額を引き上げて利率を人為的に低くすれば好況が始まり、人々が安いローンを組むことを助長する。❹しばらくすると、利率が市場レベルに戻り、人々は付加利子のついた貸付金のすべてを払う余裕があるわけではないことに気がつく。❺彼らは支出をやめ、生産は下がり、不況が程なく続く。

G　❶ハイエクの考えでは、政府が赤字財政支出に従事すると、事態を悪化させるだけだ。❷銀行と会社は失敗の結果に気づかされる必要があるとハイエクは感じていた。❸もし政府が「大手なので破綻させられない」とみなされる銀行や会社の救済に介入すれば、彼らは本質的に自らの行動が招いた結果を容認されることになる。そうして、こうした銀行や会社は同じ過ちを繰り返し、さらに補助金を求めて戻って来続ける可能性がある。❹ハイエクの支持者達は、持続不能な好況から転じた不況に痛みを伴わない回復はないと強調した。❺痛みを伴わない唯一の方法は、好況そのものを避けることだ。

H　❶ケインズは財政危機の間の政府の措置の必要性を信じていたので、ハイエクは何もしないことが良いと信じていたのだとよく考えられているが、これは誤りだ。❷技術革新と成長を刺激するために企業への規制を撤廃し、なおかつ、家庭と企業が支出や投資をするための資金をより多く持てるように税金の負担を軽くするという観点で、回復を支援するために政府にはやるべきことが多くあると彼は感じていた。

I　❶ハイエクの緊縮型のアプローチよりも、ケインズの財政出動の考えに人々は魅了され、ケインズの考えが大恐慌の時代に適用されるものとなった。❷彼は、ルーズベルト大統領のニュー・ディール政策の後ろ盾となる理論を提供して、大恐慌を終結させることに助力した功績があると一般に考えられている。❸人々がハイエクに

本格的に注目し始めたのは第二次大戦の数年後になってからだったが、そうなるや
ハイエクの思想が支配的となった。❹ハイエクは1974年にノーベル経済学賞を受
賞し、彼の思想は1980年代のアメリカ合州国の金融政策で実行に移された。

重要語句

☐ **in that ...**	〔熟〕	…という点で
☐ **deficit spending**	〔名〕	赤字財政支出
☐ **aggregate demand**	〔名〕	総需要
☐ **as opposed to ...**	〔熟〕	…に対して
☐ **magnum opus**	〔名〕	最高傑作
☐ **vicious cycle**	〔名〕	悪循環
☐ **virtuous cycle**	〔名〕	好循環
☐ **interest rates**	〔名〕	利率
☐ **accrue**	〔動〕	（当然の結果として）生じる
☐ **austere**	〔形〕	厳しい
☐ **be credited with ...**	〔熟〕	…で高い評価を得る

正解一覧

1 I **2** E **3** G **4** B **5** D **6** H
7 collapse in investment **8** underemployment equilibrium
9 boom **10** market **11** TRUE
12 FALSE **13** NOT GIVEN

問題文和訳

Questions 1–6

本文はA–Iの9段落である。
以下の情報を含むのはどの段落か？
解答用紙の解答欄1–6にA–Iの正しい文字を記入しなさい。

1 ケインズの考えは必然的にハイエクの考えより魅力的だった。
2 不況に対抗するには、支出することが政府の責任だ。
3 他の銀行が教訓を得ることができるように過剰支出の銀行を破綻させる
　　ことが重要だ。
4 大恐慌が約10年続いた。

5　ハイエクは政府の支出より個人の投資を見ることを好んだ。

6　ハイエクは政府には税金を減らす責任があると考えた。

1　‖正解‖ I

I段落1文 People were more attracted to Keynes' ideas of spending than they were to Hayek's more austere approach（ハイエクの緊縮型のアプローチよりも、ケインズの財政出動の考えに人々は魅了され）に該当する。

2　‖正解‖ E

E段落4文 it was the government's job to increase its own spending to reverse the decline in consumer spending（消費者支出の下落を逆転するために支出を増やすことが政府の仕事だった）の言及があり、jobがresponsibilityに該当する。

3　‖正解‖ G

G段落2文 Hayek felt that banks and companies had to be made aware of the consequences of failure（銀行と会社は失敗の結果に気づかされる必要があるとハイエクは感じていた）の「失敗を気づかせる」は「破綻させる」ことを指す。

4　‖正解‖ B

B段落1文に The Great Depression was a severe downturn that affected much of the world in the decade ...（大恐慌は、…10年間で世界の大部分に影響をもたらした厳しい景気低迷の期間だった）という記述がある。

5　‖正解‖ D

D段落2、4文 Saw the economy not as a government-dominated enterprise but as a collection of individuals engaging in production and trade（経済を政府主導の事業ではなく、生産と商売に従事する個人の集まりと見なした）と private investment would promote sustainable growth（民間の投資が持続可能な成長を促進する）に該当する。

6　‖正解‖ H

H段落2文に He felt government had a lot to do in order to aid recovery ... in lightening the tax burden（税金の負担を軽くするという観点で、回復を支援するために政府にはやるべきことが多くあると彼は感じていた）という記述がある。

‖ 問題文和訳

Questions 7–10

以下の図を完成しなさい。

本文から3語以内の言葉を選び、解答用紙の解答欄7–10に解答を記入しなさい。

＜ケインズの理論＞

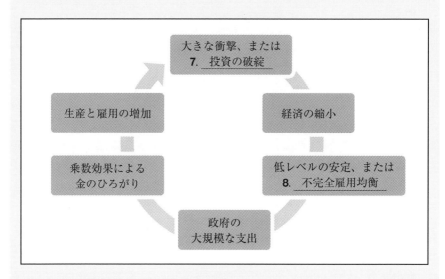

＜ハイエクの理論＞

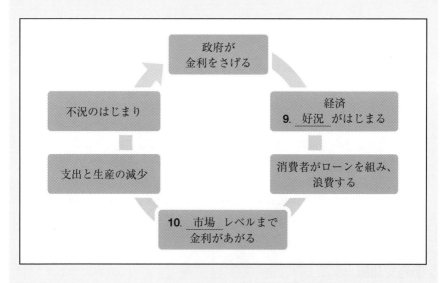

7 　正解　collapse in investment

問題文中のor（言い換えれば）に注目すると、big shock と文中で同格な内容はその例にあたるE段落2文中collapse in investment（投資の破綻）である。

8 　正解　underemployment equilibrium

E段落にケインズの理論の言及があり、とくに2文the economy would keep shrinking until it reached stability at a low level, which he called "underemployment equilibrium"（彼が「不完全雇用均衡」と呼んだ低レベルの安定に達するまで経済は縮小し続ける）の記述が、図表の流れに該当する。

9 　正解　boom

F段落にハイエクの理論が述べられており、3文The booms begin when the government or the banks expand credit or reduce interest rates to artificially low levels（政府や銀行が貸付金額を引き上げて利率を人為的に低くすれば好況が始まる）に該当し、循環の主な流れが把握できる。

10 　正解　market

F段落3文interest rates return to market levels（利率が市場レベルに戻る）とあり、人工的に下げられた利率が市場レベルに戻る（＝上がる）ことがわかる。

問題文和訳

Questions 11–13

以下の文は本文で与えられた情報に一致するか？
解答用紙の空欄11–13の欄に次のように書きなさい。

TRUE 　　もし情報と一致すれば
FALSE 　情報と矛盾すれば
NOT GIVEN 　これに関する情報がなければ

11 経済は自然発生的に下落から回復しないだろうとケインズは考えた。
12 ケインズは政府の役割は、経済苦境時に消費を抑えることだと信じた。
13 ハイエクは、銀行制度は完全に再編成されるべきだと感じた。

11 　正解　TRUE

E段落にケインズの理論が述べられており、2文He thought that there was no automatic force for recovery in a market economy ...（市場経済には自

然発生的な回復力がない…と彼は考えた）に該当する。

12 |正解| **FALSE**

C段落2文でケインズは赤字からの回復は政府が支出することで解決する、と逆の主張をしているので本文と矛盾する。

13 |正解| **NOT GIVEN**

G段落にハイエクの銀行制度に対する考えが述べられており、2文で「銀行や会社に失敗を気付かせる必要がある」という言及はあるが、「再編成する」という記述はない。

*You should spend about 20 minutes on **Questions 1–13,** which are based on the reading passage below.*

Learning in the East and West

The English poet Rudyard Kipling once famously wrote, 'East is East and West is West, and never the twain shall meet'. Yet as China grows increasingly prosperous, Chinese students can be found in universities all over the Western world, often doing well in their studies, while the West is increasingly looking for lessons to learn from China's rapid rise. When the modern Easterner meets the modern Westerner, each carries within them the cultural influence of their forebears; the Confucian endeavour and respect for elders in the former, and the Socratic search for self-knowledge in the latter.

Now a Chinese writer, Jin Li, a professor at Brown University in the United States who is steeped in both traditions, has illuminated the cultural differences in learning with her book 'Cultural Foundations of Learning: East and West'. She concludes that one reason for the success of the East Asian students is that they work much harder than American students do. However, the reason they work so hard is complex, and relates to very different ideas between Western and Asian notions of learning and development.

East Asian children are brought up under a Confucian tradition that emphasises perseverance. When a child in China or other countries within the Confucian tradition does well, the parents do not respond with the effusive praise that is common in the West. Instead, they turn the child's attention toward further acts of self-study. In a study comparing discussions of learning among parents in Europe and America with those in Taiwan, Li found that the former tended to use words like 'fun' or 'pride', while the latter referred to the need to persevere through pain on the way to future accomplishments. Moreover, Taiwanese adults teach their children the virtues that lead to successful lifelong learning: a sense of humility, respect for parents and teachers, and a celebration of hard-working peers. Failure to develop these moral strengths can lead to familial shame.

Of course Westerners also want their children to develop a love for learning, but tend to worry that trying to control the direction their children take will weaken their natural curiosity. When intrinsic interest fails, parents and teachers attempt to motivate learning by making it interesting or fun. If these attempts also fail, Americans tend to use external incentives, such as rewards and punishments.

At the heart of this difference lie two concepts of what it means to grow as a person: in Chinese society, personhood must be developed through the continuous cultivation of moral virtues including respect for the family, modesty, and celebration of achievement. In contrast, American society is organised around the primacy of the individual expressed in values such as independence, self-expression, and the pursuit of happiness. Thus, for Western students, learning is not morally based behaviour but rather a practical activity performed to attain outcomes like grades, jobs, or status.

From the perspective of many Westerners, the Chinese advantage in education comes at too high a cost. Westerners place less emphasis on social hierarchy, familial honour, or proper social behaviour. However, there is some convergence. The concept of moral self-cultivation, for example, is compatible with the Aristotelian concepts, since Aristotle saw happiness, the ultimate target of human activities, as achievable only by cultivating moral goodness over the course of a lifetime. The compatibility between East Asian notions of self-cultivation and Western concepts of self-improvement illustrates the danger of accepting simple explanations wholesale.

Another notable expert on this subject is Jim Stigler, a professor of psychology at the University of California, Los Angeles who has studied the learning mindset of Eastern and Western students. As a graduate student at the University of Michigan, Stigler visited Japan to research training methods, and sat in on a fourth-grade math class where the children were attempting to draw three-dimensional cubes on paper. One of the students was having more trouble than the others, so the teacher encouraged that student to come up to the board and try to draw a cube in front of the class. The Japanese student did so, but still couldn't create the cube. However, the kid persevered, and by the end of the class he had created the correct form of cube, to general applause. Stigler surmised that in an

American classroom it would have been the best kid in the class who was asked to demonstrate on the board, and the kid would be applauded according to the ease with which he accomplished the task.

Stigler sees this as indicating a very different approach to the concept of 'struggle' between the East and West. In the West, smart people are expected to be a 'quick study', and struggling may indicate that the student is not very smart. In East Asian cultures, on the other hand, struggling is a part of the learning process, and through struggling the student demonstrates that he or she has what it takes to persevere. Granted that there is a lot of cultural diversity within the East and West, Stigler sums up the difference this way: for the most part in Western cultures, intellectual struggle in schoolchildren is seen as an indicator of weakness, while in Eastern cultures it is used to measure emotional strength.

Eastern students' attitudes to perseverance can also be demonstrated by a study that Stigler carried out with first-grade students. He and his team gave the students an impossible math problem and recorded how long they worked on it. The American students studied it for less than half a minute on average before informing Stigler that they hadn't learned how to solve such problems. However, the Japanese students worked on the experiment for the entire hour allotted to them. The obvious implication, of course, is that Eastern students will approach their problems with greater drive. A kinder interpretation is that the Americans might target their thinking efficiently, leaving them time to focus on other matters.

Questions 1–6

Look at the following statements (Questions 1-6) and the list of people below.

*Match each statement with the correct person, **A–E**.*

*Write the correct letter, **A–E**, in boxes 1–6 on your answer sheet.*

***NB** You may use any letter more than once.*

1   developed a philosophy that encourages perseverance and hard work

2   concluded that an important part of learning involved overcoming problems

3   implied there was an unbridgeable gap between Asian and Western cultures

4   compared how parents from different cultures support their child's learning

5   observed that cultural differences can shape a child's determination

6   believed that happiness was only achievable by developing moral strength

A	Jim Stigler
B	Rudyard Kipling
C	Jin Li
D	Aristotle
E	Confucius

*Choose the correct letter, **A, B, C** or **D**.*

Write your answers in boxes 7–9 on your answer sheet.

7 Jin Li found that East Asian students tend to

   A be influenced by the Socratic tradition.

   B study harder than Westerners.

   C congregate at Brown or UCLA universities.

   D emphasise having fun in the classroom.

8 In a Japanese classroom, the child who couldn't perform the task

   A practised drawing in front of the entire class.

   B became demotivated and stopped trying.

   C watched a demonstration from the ablest student.

   D kept trying because his friends offered encouragement.

9 When given an unachievable math task, the American students

   A each worked in an individual way.

   B discovered the answer with great efficiency.

   C gave up almost as soon as they began.

   D worked on the task for half an hour.

Questions 10–13

*Complete the summary using the list of words, **A–P**, below.*
*Write the correct letter, **A–P**, in boxes 10–13 on your answer sheet.*

Despite Kipling's comments that East and West shall never meet, East Asians and Westerners are constantly interacting. Yet their very different traditions mean that they think about the process of learning differently. Jin Li has written a book on the reasons for this. She writes that East Asian children are brought up in an environment that stresses the virtue of **10** _____. From an early age, Chinese parents, instead of praising the child's accomplishment, indicate the need for more study. Meanwhile, Western parents try hard to make learning fun, and think that forcing their child to study will destroy the child's **11** _____. This reflects the Eastern idea of learning as a moral act as opposed to the Western preference for making learning fun and using **12** _____. Jim Stigler noted how Japanese classrooms paid attention to the weakest student while American ones focused on the strongest. He also carried out an experiment in which Japanese students persevered in the face of a(n) **13** _____ problem.

A impatience	**B** intelligence	**C** disrespect	**D** impossible
E improbable	**F** curiosity	**G** hope	**H** depression
I wisdom	**J** incentives	**K** elation	**L** altruism
M perseverance	**N** unlikely	**O** irritable	**P** Confucian

Exercise 12　解答解説

全文訳

東西の学習

1 ❶英国の詩人ラドヤード・キップリングはかつて周知の通りこのように書いた。「東は東、西は西。2つが合一することは決してない」。❷しかし、中国がますます繁栄するにつれ、中国人学生が西洋世界全域の大学で見受けられるようになり学業が優秀であることがよくあると同時に、西洋は中国の急速な台頭から教訓を探すことが増えている。❸現代の東洋人が現代の西洋人に会う時、それぞれが先祖の文化的影響を有している；前者においては儒教的な努力と年長者に対する敬意、後者においてはソクラテス式自己認識の追求である。

2 ❶中国人の作家チン・リーはアメリカ合衆国のブラウン大学で教授をしていて、彼女は両方の伝統にどっぷり浸かってきたのだが、その著書『学習の文化的基盤：東洋と西洋』の中で、学習における文化の違いについて明らかにしている。❷東アジアの学生の成功の一つの理由として、アメリカ人学生よりずっと懸命に学習しているからだと結論づけている。❸しかし、かれらがとても懸命に勉強する理由は複雑であり、それは学習と成長に対する西洋とアジアの概念の間にある非常に大きな考え方の違いと関連がある。

3 ❶東アジアの子供達は忍耐を強調する儒教の伝統のもとで育てられる。❷儒教の伝統を持つ中国や他の国々の子供の成績が良い時、両親は西洋ではありがちな感情をあらわにした称賛で反応することはない。❸そうではなく、さらなる自習行動に子供の関心を向ける。❹ヨーロッパとアメリカの両親と台湾の両親の間の学習についての議論を比較する調査で、前者は「おもしろさ」や「誇り」のような言葉を使用する傾向があり、一方で後者は将来の達成に向かう途上での苦しみに耐える必要性に言及するということにリーは気づいた。❺さらに、台湾の大人は、謙虚さ、両親と教師に対する尊敬、勉強熱心な仲間への賞賛といった、生涯学習の成功に通じる美徳を子供に教える。❻このような道徳的な強みを発達させることができないと、一族の恥につながることもある。

4 ❶もちろん西洋人も子供達に学習愛を身につけてほしいと思っているが、子供達がたどる方向をコントロールしようとすることは、子供達が生来持っている好奇心を弱めることになると心配する傾向がある。❷生まれ持った関心が出てこない時は、両親や教師は興味深くしたり面白くしたりすることで学習の動機づけを試みる。❸もしこれらの

試みも失敗したら、アメリカ人はほうびや罰のような外的な刺激を使う傾向がある。

5 ❶こうした違いの中心にあるのが、人間としての成長が意味することに対する2つ
の概念である：中国社会では、人間性というものは孝行の徳、謙遜、達成の称賛を含む
道徳的な美徳の継続的な育成を通して身につけなくてはいけない。❷対照的に、自立、
自己表現、幸福の追求のような価値観で表される個人の重要性を中心にアメリカ社会は
編成されている。❸ゆえに、西洋人学生にとって学習は道徳に基づく行為ではなく、む
しろ成績、仕事、地位のような成果を達成するために行われる実際的な活動である。

6 ❶多くの西洋人の視点からすれば、教育における中国人の利点はあまりにも大きな
代償がある。❷社会的序列、一族の名誉、適切な社会行為に西洋人はあまり重きを置か
ない。❸しかし、合致する部分もある。❹例えば、道徳的自己修養の概念はアリストテ
レスの概念と両立可能だ。なぜなら、アリストテレスは人間の活動の究極の目標である
幸福を生涯にわたり道徳的な美徳を育成することによってのみ達成できると見なしてい
た。❺東アジアの自己修養の考えと西洋人の自己改善の概念の間の両立性は、単純な説
明を見境なく認めることの危険を明らかにしている。

7 ❶この話題に関するもう一人の有名な専門家がUCLAの心理学科教授のジム・ス
ティグラーで、彼は東西の学生の学習態度を研究している。❷ミシガン大学の大学院生
だった時、スティグラーは教育法を研究するために日本を訪問し、4年生の数学の授業
を参観したが、そこで子供達は紙に立方体を描こうとしていた。❸1人の生徒がとくに
困っていたので、教師はその生徒に黒板に出てきてクラスの前で立方体を描くように促
した。❹その日本人生徒は従ったが、それでもうまく立方体にならなかった。❺しかし、
その子供はやり抜いて、授業の終わりまでには正しい形の立方体を描き、全員の拍手を
あびた。❻アメリカの教室ならば黒板に出て実演するように求められるのはクラスで一
番良くできる生徒であり、拍手をあびるとすれば課題をいともたやすく行うからだとス
ティグラーは推測した。

8 ❶このことは、奮闘という概念に対する東西の異なる捉え方を示しているとスティ
グラーは見なしている。❷西洋では、賢い人々なら「速習者」であることが期待され、
奮闘しているならその学生があまり賢くないことを示すことになるだろう。❸他方、東
アジアの文化では、奮闘することは学習過程の一部であり、奮闘を通して学生はやり通
すことに必要な資質を持っていることを示す。❹仮に東西に多くの文化の多様性が存在
するとしても、違いは次のようになるとスティグラーはまとめている：たいてい西洋文
化では生徒の学習上の奮闘は欠点の指標であり、一方で東洋文化では心の強さを測るた
めに使われる。

9 ❶忍耐に対する東洋の学生の姿勢は、スティグラーが1年生の生徒で行なった研究でも例証できる。❷彼と彼のチームは、生徒に解答不可能な数学の問題を出し、どのくらいの時間生徒が取り組むのかを記録した。❸アメリカ人生徒が取り組んだ時間は平均30秒以下で、すぐにそのような問題の解き方を学んでないとスティグラーに知らせた。❹しかしながら、日本人生徒は割り当てられた丸1時間を使ってその実験に取り組んだ。❺言うまでもなく、東洋の学生が多大な意欲で課題に取り組むことを明らかに示している。❻西洋に対してひいき目に解釈するならば、アメリカ人は効率的に思考の対象を定めて、他の問題に集中する時間を確保しているのかもしれない。

注：アメリカ人は「アジア人」という言葉を中国人、日本人、韓国人のような人々を述べるために使用する傾向がある一方で、英国では概してインド、パキスタン、バングラデシュを意味する。それでここでは「東アジア人」という語を用いている。

重要語句

☐ **forebear**	〔名〕	先祖
☐ **former**	〔形〕	前者の
☐ **latter**	〔形〕	後者の
☐ **be steeped in ...**	〔熟〕	に染まっている
☐ **perseverance**	〔名〕	忍耐
☐ **effusive**	〔形〕	感情をあらわにした
☐ **incentive**	〔名〕	刺激、動機
☐ **hierarchy**	〔名〕	社会的階級
☐ **granting that ...**	〔熟〕	仮に…だと認めるとしても
☐ **(be) allotted to ...**	〔熟〕	…に割り当てられる

正解一覧

1 E	**2** A	**3** B	**4** C	**5** A
6 D	**7** B	**8** A	**9** C	**10** M
11 F	**12** J	**13** D		

問題文和訳

Questions 1-6

以下の項目と人物のリストを見なさい。

Exercise 12 Learning in the East and West

それぞれの項目をそれに関連する人と一致させなさい。

解答用紙の1–6の欄にA–Eの正しい文字を記入しなさい。

解答の選択肢を2回以上使用しても良い。

1　…は忍耐と勤勉を奨励する哲学を発展させた

2　…は学習の重要な部分には問題の克服が含まれると結論づけた

3　…はアジアと西洋の文化には歴然とした隔たりがあることを示唆した

4　…はどのように異なる文化出身の親たちが子供の学習支援をするのか比較した

5　…は文化的な違いが子供の決意を形成する可能性があることを観察によって確認した

6　…は道徳的な長所を発展させることによってのみ幸福が達成できると信じた

A　ジム・スティグラー

B　ラドヤード・キップリング

C　チン・リー

D　アリストテレス

E　孔子

1　|正解|　E

2段落で東アジアの学生がアメリカ人学生よりも勤勉であることが取り上げられ、3段落1文にa Confucian tradition that emphasises perseverance（忍耐を強調する儒教の伝統）とある。儒教の伝統の創始者としてEの孔子が選べる。

2　|正解|　A

問題の克服の具体例として、苦労して立方体を描けるようになった日本の小学生や解答不可能な問題に対する日米の学生の反応などが7～9段落で挙げられている。こうしたことを考察した専門家として名前が言及されているのはスティグラーだ。

3　|正解|　B

1段落1文のキップリングの言葉の引用部分と同じ内容だとわかる。

4　|正解|　C

3段落4文でa study comparing discussions of learning among parents in Europe and America with those in Taiwan（ヨーロッパとアメリカの両親と台湾の両親の間の学習についての議論を比較する調査）を行なった人物と

してリーの名前が上がっている。

5 　正解　**A**

8段落で西洋の学生よりも東洋の学生の方がgreater drive（多大な意欲）を
もって難問に取り組もうとすることに言及があるが、実験によってそのような結論に達したのはスティグラーである。

6 　正解　**D**

6段落4文にAristotle saw happiness … as achievable only by cultivating
moral goodness（アリストテレスは…幸福を…道徳的な美徳を育成することによってのみ達成できると見なしていた）という記述部分がある。

問題文和訳

Questions 7–9

A, B, C, Dから適切なものを選びなさい。
解答用紙の7–9の解答欄に解答を記入しなさい。

7 チン・リーは東アジアの学生は…傾向があると気づいた。
- **A** ソクラテスの伝統に影響を受けている
- **B** 西洋人より懸命に学ぶ
- **C** ブラウン大学やUCLA大学に集まる
- **D** 教室内で楽しむことを強調する

8 日本のある教室で、課題が出来なかった子供が
- **A** クラス全体の前で描く練習をした。
- **B** やる気をなくし挑戦するのをやめた。
- **C** もっとも有能な生徒の実演を見つめた。
- **D** 友達が励ましたので挑戦し続けた。

9 解決不可能な数学の課題を与えられた時、アメリカ人の学生は
- **A** それぞれが自分の方法で取り組んだ。
- **B** とても効率良く解答を見つけた。
- **C** 始めてすぐにあきらめた。
- **D** 30分間その課題に取り組んだ。

7 　正解　**B**

2段落2文後半で、東アジアの学生についてthey work much harder than
American students do（アメリカ人学生よりずっと懸命に学習している）と

ある。

8　|正解|　A

7段落3文に the teacher encouraged that student to come up to the board and try to draw a cube in front of the class（教師はその生徒に黒板に出てきてクラスの前で立方体を描くように促した）とあるのでAが正解。

9　|正解|　C

9段落3文に The American students studied it for less than half a minute on average（アメリカ人生徒が取り組んだ時間は平均30秒以下だった）とあるので、「すぐにやめた」Cが正解。Dは「30分間」なので誤り。

問題文和訳

Questions 10–13

欄内のA–Pの語のリストを使って要約を完成しなさい。
解答用紙の10–13の欄にA–Pのうち、正しいものを記入しなさい。

東洋と西洋は決して合一することがないだろうというキップリングの言葉にもかかわらず、東アジアと西洋の人々はたえず交流している。しかし、かれらの非常に異なる伝統は、学習方法についての考え方が異なることを意味する。チン・リーはこの理由についての本を書いた。東アジアの子供達は **10** 忍耐 の美徳を強調するように育てられると書いている。幼い時期から、中国の親は、子供の達成をほめる代りに、もっと勉強する必要性を示す。その一方で、西洋の親は学習を楽しくするように働きかけ、子供に勉強を強いることは子供の **11** 好奇心 を壊すのだと考える。これは、学習を道徳的行動ととらえる東洋の考えに対して、学習を楽しいものにして **12** 刺激 を利用することを好む西洋の傾向を反映している。ジム・スティグラーは日本の教室が一番の劣等生に注目する一方で、アメリカの教室はもっとも優秀な生徒に焦点を当てている様子に注目した。また彼は実験を行なったところ、日本人生徒が **13** 解答不可能な 問題に直面した時にやり抜くという結果になった。

A　いらだち	B　知性	C　無礼	D　不可能な
E　ありそうにない	F　好奇心	G　希望	H　うつ
I　知恵	J　刺激	K　高揚感	L　利他主義
M　忍耐	N　ありそうにない	O　怒りっぽい	P　儒学者

10 |正解| **M**

3段落1文とほぼ同じ内容であることからperseveranceが正解。stressは emphasiseの同義表現で「強調する」の意味。

11 |正解| **F**

4段落1文の西洋人の親の子供に対する考えの記述部分will weaken their natural curiosityに該当する。

12 |正解| **J**

4段落2~3文に、子供の学習の動機づけとして西洋の親が取る行動として use external incentives, such as rewards and punishments（ほうびや罰 のような外的な刺激を使う）が言及されている。

13 |正解| **D**

9段落2~4文で「日本人とアメリカ人生徒にimpossible math problem（数 学の解答不可能な問題）を出して、取り組む時間を比較する実験」について 述べられている。improbable, unlikely, irritable は「起こりそうにない、あ りそうにない、怒りっぽい」なので正解にはならない。

第3章

リーディング実戦模試

time: 20 minutes

You should spend about 20 minutes on **Questions 1–13,** *which are based on Reading Passage 1 below.*

The Spirit Level of Social Harmony

A   Modern societies are beset by a variety of social ills. Obesity, drugs, mental illness and street crime are just a few of the maladies that plague developed nations. And as soon as one plight is remedied another seems to rear its ugly head. In most cases these problems are treated as disparate from one another. Obesity, for example, is considered to be a health issue, while illegal drugs fall under the auspices of law enforcement agencies. Two British academics, however, claim to have unearthed the root cause behind many of these social problems, and their findings call for a serious overhaul of the more conventional approaches.

B   Richard Wilkinson, a retired medical school professor, and Kate Pickett, a university lecturer, believe that the majority of social ills in industrialised countries can be attributed to inequality, specifically the income gap between the rich and the poor. According to their theory, it is not just the underprivileged who suffer from this inequity but all levels of society. Thus, a fairer distribution of wealth, a metaphorical spirit level, can advance social cohesion and harmony.

C   An extensive body of statistics underpins their hypothesis. Obesity was found to be six times more common in the US than in a more egalitarian society such as Japan and twice as common in the UK as the more 'equal' Nordic countries. Similarly, teenage pregnancy was six times higher; mental illness three times more common; and, murder rates three times higher in countries with more pronounced income gaps.

D   These observations first came to light when Wilkinson analysed medical data and discovered that health was determined by relative differences in wealth rather than a person's absolute wealth. Later, using data released by the World Bank he uncovered similar patterns in other areas of social policy. For example, countries where the top 20% of people earn eight or nine times more than the lowest 20% experienced disproportionately higher levels of social problems than more egalitarian societies. Using data from 23 rich countries, he replicated his findings and confirmed that social problems were three to 10 times more common in more unequal societies.

E　To ensure these findings were not due to cultural factors, the same analysis was performed using data from 50 US states and exactly the same trends were discovered. Namely, in states where income differentials were largest, social ills and poor social cohesion were more prevalent. While some anomalies appeared, for example, suicide and smoking levels were higher in more equal societies, the correlations between inequality and social problems persisted. The critical factor remained the differential between the richest and poorest members rather than baseline measurements of poverty.

F　One explanation for this phenomenon lies in the psycho-social area of hierarchy and status. If there is a larger gap between the haves and have-nots, there is a greater value placed on wealth and material possessions. The kind of car you drive carries greater significance in a more hierarchical society than a flatter one. This in turn fuels status anxiety that finds expression in socially corrosive practices such as crime, ill-health and mistrust. The link between violence and inequality is well-established. Psychological studies have shown that men value status more and because of their sexually competitive nature resort to violence when their status is threatened, particularly when there is little to defend. This has been linked to evolutionary processes and the importance of shame and humiliation in terms of explaining why unequal societies suffer from more violence.

G　Wilkinson and Pickett have repeatedly tested their findings, questioning whether or not they may have overlooked anything. They

第3章

TEST

factored in religious differences and levels of multiculturalism but in all cases the results remained the same. They even considered that social problems were not driving social inequality, but found that their statistical analysis failed to support such a premise.

H   Inequality acts like an equal-opportunity disease that blights all levels of society. This raises a counter intuitive notion that aligns moral or altruistic goals with motives of self-interest. It also overturns the Hobbesian view that every member of society is locked in an eternal struggle for dominance. Instead, it advances a model of greater cooperation and support that is underpinned by unequivocal evidence.

I   Although the root cause has been uncovered, the solution remains elusive. Wilkinson feels that it is now up to others to work out the answer. One of his suggestions is that governments should limit pay at the top end. Whether they are likely to do so or not is another matter altogether. Pickett, on the other hand, stresses the importance of campaigning for change. In particular, she believes that reducing inequality will benefit the environmental agenda. It would also benefit those in the developing world as equal societies typically give more assistance in terms of overseas aid. In a zeitgeist where people are increasingly fed up with corporate greed their revelation comes at an opportune time to challenge both the dominant ideology and the political will of our leaders.

Questions 1–5

Do the following statements agree with the information given in Reading Passage 1?

In boxes 1–5 on your answer sheet, write

TRUE *if the statement agrees with the information*

FALSE *if the statement contradicts the information*

NOT GIVEN *if there is no information on this*

1　Wealth is more evenly distributed in Japan than in America.

2　Obesity is the largest public health menace.

3　Adolescent mothers are more common in unequal societies.

4　Baseline poverty proved to be a critical factor behind many social problems.

5　Figures from the World Bank were readily available.

Questions 6–10

Reading Passage 1 has nine paragraphs, **A–I**.

Which paragraph contains the following information?

*Write the correct letter, **A–I**, in boxes 6–10 on your answer sheet.*

NB *You may use any letter more than once.*

6　The original study that gave birth to the theory

7　An international comparison of public health issues

8　Negative outcomes for egalitarian societies

9　Proof their findings were not explainable by cultural differences

10　A concept that links compassion and selfishness

第3章

TEST

Answer the questions below.

*Choose **NO MORE THAN THREE WORDS** from the passage for each answer.*

Write your answers in boxes 11–13 on your answer sheet.

11   What data initially triggered the 'Spirit Level' hypothesis?

12   What social problems are more prevalent in egalitarian societies?

13   What assistance is likely to increase as a result of societies becoming more egalitarian?

第3章

TEST

NO TEST MATERIAL ON THIS PAGE

*You should spend about 20 minutes on **Questions 14–26,** which are based on Reading Passage 2 below.*

The Olympic Games

Ancient historical records trace the first Olympic Games as far back as 776 BCE. The ancient games took place among imposing temples to the gods at the scenic site of Olympia, situated in a valley in the western Peloponnese. The city-states of Greece were often at war, so a truce was announced before and after each Games to ensure the host city was not attacked, and that athletes and spectators could travel safely to the Games before returning to their respective countries in peace. During the truce period, which lasted up to three months, wars and legal disputes were suspended and death penalties forbidden. The Olympic Games aimed to showcase the physical abilities of the sportsmen who took part, as well as encouraging good relations among the cities of Greece. Although Olympia itself was dominated by a temple to Zeus and religious ceremonies took place during the festivities, the Games themselves were secular in character.

All free male Greek citizens, regardless of social status, were entitled to participate in the ancient Olympic Games. Women were not allowed to join in, but, unmarried women were allowed to watch the competition. After each race of the Games was won, the winner's name would be announced, and a judge would place a palm branch in his hands while the spectators cheered and threw flowers to him. Red ribbons were also tied on his head and hands as a mark of victory. The official award ceremony would take place at the temple of Zeus on the last day of the Games. The announcer would declare the name of each winner, his father's name, and his homeland, then a sacred olive tree wreath would be placed on the winner's head.

The ancient Olympic Games were held every four years as a one-day event until 684 BCE, when they were extended to three days. In the 5th century BCE the Games were lengthened again to cover five days. The ancient Games included wrestling, boxing, long jump, javelin and discus throwing, and chariot racing.

The discus event was very similar to the one we know today, but the long jump was a little different, with the competitors holding onto weights to give them extra distance. Another notable event was the pentathlon, which comprised the five events of running, wrestling, javelin throwing, discus throwing, and long jump. The hardest race of all was for the citizen-soldiers known as hoplites, who would run while wearing armour and carrying shields.

Two other main martial sports were wrestling and boxing. Wrestling was highly valued as a form of military exercise, and ended only when one of the contestants admitted defeat. Boxing got more extreme over time, as the leather straps that the boxers wrapped around their hands to strengthen their wrists and steady their fingers, initially soft, got harder and ended up disfiguring their opponents' faces. Another martial sport was the pankration, a combination of wrestling and boxing that was considered to be one of the toughest forms of fighting. Greeks believed that it was founded by Theseus when he defeated the fierce Minotaur, a bull-headed monster, in the labyrinth. Finally, the Olympics featured equestrian events including horse and chariot races that took place in an open arena known as a hippodrome.

The Olympic Games continued unbroken for a full 12 centuries, and many wonderful athletes competed in the stadium and hippodrome of ancient Olympia's sacred area. Some became legends by winning in successive Games and staying at the top of their sport for decades. Milon, a pupil of Pythagoras who came from the Greek city of Croton in southern Italy, was one of the most famous of all. He was crowned Olympic wrestling champion no fewer than six times, winning his first event at the 60th Olympiad in 540 BCE, and continuing to win until finally losing to a younger competitor at the 67th Olympiad in 512 BCE. Leonidas of Rhodes (164–152 BCE) also achieved fame for winning three races in each of four consecutive Olympiads, thereby garnering a total of 12 Olympic victory wreaths. He was acclaimed as a hero by his countrymen.

For nearly 1,200 years the ancient Olympic Games thrived until 393 CE, when the Roman emperor Theodosius I, a Christian, abolished them because of their pagan influences. After languishing for more than 1,500 years, the ideals of the Olympics were revived by three key figures: Evangelis Zappas in Greece, William Brookes in the UK, and Pierre de Coubertin in France. Zappas and

第3章

TEST

Brookes didn't know one another, but as enthusiasts of classical literature they both admired a Greek poet named Dimitris Soutsos, who had appealed for a modern Olympics, and it was this appeal that inspired both men to separately launch their own games. Zappas was a businessman who made a fortune and then used his wealth to fund the first of a series of Olympiads in Athens from 1859. Meanwhile, Brookes was producing his own games in the small town of Much Wenlock in Shropshire, England. By 1887, these had evolved to become the British Olympic Games. His games were especially noteworthy for exhibiting the first women's Olympic event. In 1881 Brookes proposed to the Greek government that the parallel games in Shropshire and Athens be internationalised. This idea was taken up by de Coubertin, who did much to organise the first truly international events that began in Paris in 1896.

Questions 14–18

*Choose the correct letter, **A, B, C** or **D**.*

Write your answers in boxes 14–18 on your answer sheet

14 According to the passage, which of the following would be ineligible to compete in the ancient Olympic Games?
   A An unmarried Greek farmer
   B A male citizen of the Peloponnese
   C A Greek slave
   D A member of the Greek militia

15 What prize was presented to winners in the earliest official award ceremonies?
   A An Olympic medal
   B Red ribbons
   C An olive crown
   D A garland of flowers

16 What was included as an equestrian event in the earliest Games?
   A Chariot racing
   B The pentathlon
   C Javelin
   D Discus throwing

17 What was Milon most famous for?
   A Being the wrestling champion at the first Olympiad
   B Winning his sixth crown at the 67th Olympiad
   C Winning the highest number of victory wreaths
   D Winning the same event over an extended period

18 When did the modern Olympics obtain international status?
   A 1859
   B 1887
   C 1881
   D 1896

Questions 19–23

Complete the sentences below.

Choose **ONE WORD ONLY** from the passage for each answer.

Write your answers in boxes, 19–23, on your answer sheet.

19 To ensure the safety of competitors and citizens a _____ was necessary for the duration of the Games.

20 In addition to allowing athletes to showcase their physical prowess, the ancient games were designed to boost _____ between different areas of Greece.

21 Although many of the athletic events have not changed since the ancient games, competitors no longer carry _____ to lengthen their jumps.

22 The most extreme combat sport included in the ancient Games was the _____.

23 A _____ Roman emperor stopped the Games in the 4th century CE because of his religious beliefs.

Questions 24–26

Complete each sentence with the correct ending, **A–F**, below.

Write the correct letter, **A–F**, in boxes 24–26 on your answer sheet.

24 Wrestling and boxing were valued because they

25 Equestrian events in ancient Greece

26 The British Olympic Games

A were held in the hippodrome.

B introduced the first events for women.

C were believed to have been founded by Theseus.

D developed important military skills.

E continued unbroken for 12 centuries.

第3章

TEST

NO TEST MATERIAL ON THIS PAGE

*You should spend about 20 minutes on **Questions 27–40**, which are based on Reading Passage 3 below.*

The Return of the Wolf

The once-ubiquitous wolf has been hunted almost to extinction in many parts of Europe and North America. For centuries, wolves were considered dangerous pests, and killing them was often a good way for hunters to earn bounties. Medieval English kings would even make land grants on the condition that the recipients carried out wolf hunts. In Western Europe, the wolves faced shrinking habitats as the human population expanded, and people cut down the forests and ate the animals that the wolves depended on. As a result, wolves disappeared from almost all of Western Europe, although a few clung on in Italy and Spain.

In the United States, English pioneers made great efforts to wipe out the abundant wolves that began feasting on their livestock almost from the moment the colonists established a presence in Jamestown. These efforts escalated, and in the 1850s Utah was spending more than 10% of its budget on killing wolves. Yet every fairy tale has a happy ending, and now the creature that often played the villain in cautionary tales for children—think Little Red Riding Hood—and was the stuff of nightmares is staging a comeback. Big bad humanity has come to see the error of its ways, and is now trying to conserve rather than destroy the wolf.

This turnaround is partly due to the long-term movement of people from the countryside to the city that has led to a fall in the human population in rural areas. Meanwhile, governments have started planting trees in areas where they once exploited forests for timber, and the woodlands are expanding once more. Moreover, few people hunt wild animals, such as deer or boar, these days, and the populations of these animals are growing. All these trends are helping to make the environment suitable for the wolf's return.

People's attitudes to wolves have also been changing. In the 19th and early 20th centuries, environmentalists believed that killing wolves and other predators was

justified in order to conserve the animals that they preyed upon. But Aldo
Leopold, an influential figure in America's conservation movement, disagreed.
He pointed out that the disappearance of wolves from an area would often change
it for the worse, as the expanding numbers of deer and other prey that the wolf
previously kept in check would eat all the small trees and seedlings in the forests.

The movement of people from the countryside to the city has also led to a more
romantic image of the wolf, which is now seen less as a dangerous killer and
more as an attractive symbol of the wilderness. In a way, it is strange that the
wolf has been demonised for so long. Bears are more dangerous—they often
attack when disturbed, whereas wolves usually run away. Changing public
attitudes have also led to legislation preventing the extinction of endangered
species, which have often included the wolf, in many European countries and in
North America.

In Europe, wolves have returned naturally, crossing from Finland into Sweden in
1977, Italy into France in 1992, and Poland into Germany, the Netherlands, and
Belgium over a 20-year period starting in the 1990s. In Europe, wolves receive
protection from the EU Habitats Directive. However, as wolves move toward
populated areas, some familiar problems are starting to re-emerge. In the
countryside of Brandenburg, Germany, where some 160 wolves live, the wolves
have killed 360 sheep in the past six years. The local government has set up a
fund to compensate the farmers for their losses, but claiming compensation is a
time-consuming bureaucratic process. Moreover, unlike North American wolves,
which travel in larger packs to improve their hunting success, German wolf packs
usually consist of parents and offspring, and these small family units tend to
wander into small towns to look for food when it is scarce elsewhere.

Although wolf numbers are growing in most of Western Europe, the population
growth is most dramatic in North America, where wolves benefit from the
combination of animal protection laws and a small human population. Unlike in
Western Europe, where wolves drifted in from countries such as Russia, the U.S.
government has actively reintroduced wolves to some areas. In 1995, 14 grey
wolves were captured in Canada and released in Yellowstone National Park and
nearby Idaho, where they quickly multiplied and have had a dramatic ecological
impact. Since their introduction, Yellowstone's elk population has fallen from

about 20,000 to 5,000, and the vegetation, especially young willow and aspen trees, has been able to flourish and reach maturity in the absence of so many grazers. Bison and beavers are also thriving in the new habitat, and the grizzly bears that scavenge off the wolf kills are doing well.

Yet not everyone supports the return of the wolf. As in Europe, farmers in America are suffering losses, and the anxiety experienced by cattle living near wolves means that the average weight of cows is dropping. Now that wolf numbers are recovering, protection has been removed in some areas, and they can be hunted in all the states around the Rocky Mountains and the Great Lakes. The problem is to keep the numbers in balance so that the cattle farmers, environment, and the wolves can jointly thrive.

Questions 27–33

*Do the following statements agree with the information given in
Reading Passage 3?*

In boxes 27–33 on your answer sheet, write

> **TRUE**   *if the statement agrees with the information*
> **FALSE**   *if the statement contradicts the information*
> **NOT GIVEN** *if there is no information on this*

27   English kings used to give a reward for each wolf skin.

28   For a while, there were no wolves in any European country.

29   The English colonists in America quickly wiped out local wolves.

30   The environmentalist Leopold thought killing wolves was justified.

31   In Germany, farmers find it difficult to get compensation for dead sheep.

32   The number of Elk in Yellowstone Park has significantly declined since 1995.

33   Cattle suffer from stress when wolves are in the vicinity.

第3章

TEST

Complete the summary below.

*Choose **ONE WORD ONLY** from the passage for each answer.*

Write your answers in boxes 34–40 on your answer sheet.

The Wolf Returns

In the past, wolves were prevalent throughout Europe and viewed as pests. As a result, wolves often had **34** _____ placed on them. In addition to being hunted, wolves had to contend with a spreading human population which gradually reduced their own **35** _____. In the United States, wolves were also hunted down mercilessly because they threatened the colonists'

36 _____.

The migration of people from the countryside to the city together with the recognition that wolves can benefit the natural environment has led to a change in attitudes, and governments in both Western Europe and the US have now passed laws to protect all **37** _____ animals, including wolves. Consequently, wolves have started returning to many European countries although they had to be **38** _____ to Yellowstone National Park in the US. These changes have proven very beneficial, especially in Yellowstone, where the reduction in elk numbers has enabled more saplings to grow to **39** _____. Yet farmers are having to accept stock losses, although they are able to apply for **40** _____ from the local authorities.

第3章

TEST

NO TEST MATERIAL ON THIS PAGE

全文訳

社会的調和の平衡基準

A ❶現代社会には様々な社会的病がつきまとう。❷肥満、ドラッグ、精神病、路上犯罪などは先進国を苦しめる病弊のほんの一部である。❸1つの苦境が改善されるやいなや、別な苦境が顕在化する。❹ほとんどの場合、こうした問題には共通点がない。❺例えば、肥満は健康の問題と考えられているが、その一方で違法ドラッグは法執行機関の管理下に置かれる。❻しかしながら、2人の英国人研究者は社会問題の多くの背後にある根本的な原因が明らかになったと主張し、彼らの発見によると従来の対処法を全面的に見直すことが要求される。

B ❶医学部の教授職を退いたリチャード・ウィルキンソンと大学講師のケイト・ピケットは、産業国における不平等、とりわけ金持ちと貧乏人の所得格差によるものが大多数の社会的病の引き金であると考えている。❷彼らの説によれば、この社会的不平等に社会的、経済的に恵まれない人々のみならず社会全体が苦しめられている。❸したがって、より公平な富の分配は隠喩的意味での平衡を測る基準であり、社会の結束や調和を促進する。

C ❶広範囲にわたる大量のデータが彼らの仮説を実証している。❷米国で肥満の発生率は日本のような平等主義的な社会の6倍で、英国内ではより「平等」な北欧と比較して2倍であることがわかっている。❸同様に、顕著に所得格差がある国々では、10代の妊娠率が6倍高く、精神病が3倍も蔓延し、殺人の発生率は3倍だ。

D ❶こうした見解は、ウィルキンソンが医療データを分析し、健康状態が個人の絶対的な豊かさよりもむしろ豊かさの相対的な差異により決定されることを突き止めて初めて明るみになった。❷後に、世界銀行により公開されたデータを使って、彼は社会政策の他の分野において似通った傾向を見出した。❸例えば、国内の上位20%の富裕層が下位20%の貧困層の8-9倍の収入を得ている場合、より平等な社会と比べて社会問題が過度に多い。❹23の裕福な国のデータを使いながら彼は自らの調査結果を検証し、社会問題がより不平等な社会では3倍から10倍多く見られることを確認した。

E ❶こうした研究結果が文化的な要因ではないことを確認するため、米国の50州の

データを使って同様の分析が行われたが、全く同じ傾向が見られた。❷すなわち、国内で所得格差が大きい州では、社会的病や乏しい社会的一体性がより蔓延していた。❸自殺率と喫煙率がより平等な社会で高いなどの多少の例外が出てきたものの、不平等と社会問題の相関関係が残った。❹決定的な要因は、貧困の基準測定値よりもむしろ富裕層と貧困層の格差にあるということである。

F　❶この現象に対する1つの説明は、社会的階級や地位の心理・社会的な部分にある。❷より大きな断絶が持てるものと持たざるものの間にあるならば、豊かさと物質的財産により大きな価値をおく。❸より階級的な社会では、平等な社会以上にどんな車に乗っているかということが非常に重要になる。❹これは次に地位の渇望をあおり、それは犯罪や不健康、不信といった社会を蝕む行為となって表れる。❺暴力と不平等の関連は十分立証されている。❻心理学の研究によると、男性は女性よりも地位に価値を置き、自分の地位が脅かされたとき、特に守るべき地位がほとんどない場合において、その性別上の優位性から暴力に訴えることが明らかになっている。❼なぜ不平等な社会ほどより多くの暴力に苦しめられるのか説明するにあたって、このことは進化の過程と恥や屈辱の重要性と関連している。

G　❶ウィルキンソンとピケットは繰り返し自分の研究結果を検証し、何か見過ごしていないか自問した。❷彼らは宗教の違いや多文化のレベルも考慮してみたが、いずれの場合も結果は同じだった。❸彼らは、社会問題が社会的不平等を煽っていない可能性を考慮することまでしてみたが、統計の分析からそのような前提は裏付けられなかった。

H　❶不平等は、社会の全ての階層を害する、誰もが感染する可能性のある病のように作用する。❷このことは、倫理的もしくは利他的な目標と自己利益という動機の融合という、常識とは逆の考えを提起する。❸これは、社会の全ての構成員は支配をめぐる闘争から永遠に逃れられないのだというホッブス的な見解を覆すものでもある。❹むしろ、明快な根拠によって実証された、より大きな協力や支援の社会モデルを推進する。

I　❶根本的な原因は判明したものの、解決策はいまだはっきりしない。❷ウィルキンソンは、他の研究者が答えを出す番だと感じている。❸彼の提案の1つには、各国の政府が収入に最高限度額を設けるべきだというものがある。❹彼らがそのようにするか否かは全く別の問題だ。❺一方、ピケットは変化を起こすための組織的活動の重要性を強調している。❻特に、不平等を減らすことが環境保護の課題のためになるだろうと彼女は考えている。❼また、通常平等な社会ほど海外支援という形で

より多くの支援をほどこすため、発展途上国の人々に利益をもたすことにもなるだろう。❽人々が企業の強欲にますます愛想をつかしている時代精神において、2人の研究による新事実は、主流派のイデオロギーと我々の指導者の政治的意志に挑戦する絶好の機会に明らかになったと言える。

重要語句

☐ **obesity**	〔名〕肥満	
☐ **underprivileged**	〔形〕社会的、経済的に恵まれない	
☐ **cohesion**	〔名〕結束、一体性	
☐ **relative**	〔形〕相対的な	
☐ **disproportionately**	〔副〕過剰に	
☐ **prevalent**	〔形〕蔓延している	
☐ **persistent**	〔形〕存続する	
☐ **corrosive**	〔形〕腐食性の、（社会や精神などを）むしばむ	
☐ **overlook**	〔動〕見過ごす	
☐ **premise**	〔名〕前提	
☐ **intuitive**	〔形〕直感の	
☐ **unequivocal**	〔形〕明快な	
☐ **elusive**	〔形〕とらえどころの無い、見つけにくい	
☐ **revelation**	〔名〕暴露	

正解一覧

1 TRUE	**2** NOT GIVEN	**3** TRUE	**4** FALSE
5 NOT GIVEN	**6** D	**7** C	**8** E
9 E	**10** H	**11** medical (data)	
12 suicide and smoking		**13** overseas aid	

問題文和訳

Questions 1–5

以下の文は本文に与えられた情報と一致するか？
解答用紙の解答欄1–5に…と書きなさい。

TRUE	もし文が情報と一致すれば
FALSE	もし文が情報に矛盾すれば

NOT GIVEN　　もしこれについての情報がなければ

1　日本ではアメリカに比べて富が公平に分配されている。
2　肥満は公衆衛生上の最大の脅威である。
3　不平等社会では10代の母親はあまり珍しくない。
4　貧困の基準値が多くの社会問題の決定要因と判明した。
5　世界銀行のデータは入手が容易である。

1　|正解| TRUE
　　C段落2文で日本と米国の比較に言及されている。
2　|正解| NOT GIVEN
　　A段落で社会の病弊の1つとして挙げられているが、最大の脅威かどうかについては述べられていない。
3　|正解| TRUE
　　C段落3文で、10代の妊娠が平等な社会に比べて6倍だとある。
4　|正解| FALSE
　　E段落4文でbaseline measurements of poverty（貧困の基準測定値）が問題なのではなく貧富の差が問題なのだと明言されている。
5　|正解| NOT GIVEN
　　D段落で世界銀行が公開している情報を基に調査したという記述があるが、入手の容易さについては言及がない。

▌問題文和訳

Questions 6–10

本文1は A–Iの9段落である。以下の情報を含むのはどの段落か？
解答用紙の解答欄6–10にA–Iの正しい文字を記入しなさい。
2回以上同じ文字を使用しても良い。

6　理論を生み出した、もとになった研究
7　公衆衛生問題の国際比較
8　平等主義社会にとってのマイナスの結果
9　彼らの理論が文化の違いでは説明不能である証拠
10　共感と利己主義の融合という概念

6　|正解| D
　　D段落1文で、医療データを分析した結果、豊かさの相対的差異が鍵である

ことを初めて突き止めたことが述べられている。

7 ‖正解‖ C
C段落で、具体的な病気等のデータの国際比較がなされている。

8 ‖正解‖ E
平等主義社会における自殺や喫煙率の高さについて言及がある。

9 ‖正解‖ E
E段落1文で、文化が要因ではないことを裏付けるためにアメリカの50州の
データを分析し、不平等社会と社会問題の関連性を再確認したことが述べら
れている。

10 ‖正解‖ H
H段落で、2つの相容れない利他的目標と自己の利益の融合という概念につ
いて触れられている。

▌問題文和訳

Questions 11–13

以下の設問に答えなさい。
それぞれ本文中の3語以内の単語で答えなさい。
解答用紙の11–13の解答欄に解答を記入しなさい。

11 平衡基準説のきっかけとなったデータは何か。
12 平等主義的社会ではどのような問題が広まっているか。
13 社会がより平等主義的になると、どのような援助が増えるだろうか。

11 ‖正解‖ medical (data)
D段落1文で、もともと医療データの分析から露見したとある。

12 ‖正解‖ suicide and smoking
E段落3文で、自殺率や喫煙率がより平等な社会で高いという指摘がなされ
ている。

13 ‖正解‖ overseas aid
最終段落7文で、社会がより平等になれば海外支援という形の援助が増える
ことが示唆されている。

第3章

解答解説

解答解説

オリンピック

1 ❶古代の歴史の記録で最初のオリンピックは西暦紀元前776年までさかのぼる。❷古代オリンピックは、西ペロポネソスの谷のオリンピアの景勝地にある神々をまつる堂々とした神殿の間で行われた。❸ギリシャの都市国家は戦争中であることがよくあったので、開催都市が攻撃されないように、また競技者や観客が試合に無事移動し、その後それぞれの故郷に平穏に帰還できることを確実にするために、オリンピックの前後に休戦が宣言された。❹その休戦期間は最大で3カ月続いたが、戦争や法的な争いは一時停止され、死刑は禁止された。❺オリンピックはギリシャの都市の間の良好な関係を奨励するだけではなく、参加したスポーツマンの身体能力を見せることを目的としていた。❻オリンピアの土地はゼウスをまつる神殿がそびえ立っていたが、祭の間宗教的な儀式が行われたが、オリンピック自体は世俗的な性質のものだった。

2 ❶ギリシャの自由市民の男性全員が社会的地位に関係なく古代オリンピックに参加する資格があった。❷女性は参加が許されていなかったが、未婚女性は競技を見ることができた。❸オリンピックのそれぞれのレースに勝つと、勝者の名前が発表され、審判が彼の手にヤシの枝を握らせ、その間観客は喝采し彼に花を投げた。❹勝利の印として赤いリボンが頭と両手に結ばれた。❺正式な授賞式がゼウスの神殿でオリンピック最終日に行われた。❻アナウンサーがそれぞれの勝者の名、父の名、故郷の名を述べてから勝者の頭に聖なるオリーブの木の冠をのせた。

3 ❶古代オリンピックは紀元前684年まで4年ごとに1日の催しとして行われ、その後3日に延長された。❷紀元前5世紀、5日に及ぶように再び延ばされた。❸古代のオリンピックにはレスリング、ボクシング、走り幅跳び、やり投げ、円盤投げ、戦車レースが含まれていた。❹円盤投げは今日私達が知っているものに非常に似ているが、走り幅跳びは少し違って、競技者は距離を伸ばすために重りを持っていた。❺もう1つの良く知られた競技は五種競技で、ランニング、レスリング、やり投げ、円盤投げ、走り幅跳びの5つの種目から成っていた。❻全ての中で最も難しいものは重装歩兵と呼ばれる市民兵士のためのもので、鎧を身につけたまま盾を持ちながら走った。

4 ❶他の2つの主な格闘技はレスリングとボクシングだった。❷レスリングは軍事演習の形として非常に重んじられ、競技者の1人が負けを認めた時のみ終了した。❸ボク

シングは時を経てより過激になり、ボクサーが手首を強化し、指を安定させるために手の周りをくるむ皮ひもは当初は柔らかかったが、だんだん硬いものになり、最後は相手の顔を変形させるものになった。❹もう1つの格闘技はパンクラティオンで、レスリングとボクシングを結びつけたもので、最もきつい形態の決闘の1つと考えられていた。❺ギリシャ人は、テセウスが迷路の中で獰猛な牛の頭を持つ怪物ミノタウロスを負かした時に、彼によってつくられた競技だと信じていた。❻最後に、オリンピックは戦車競技場として知られる屋外の場所で行われる馬と戦車競走を含む馬術競技を呼び物にした。

5 ❶オリンピックの試合は途切れることなくまる12世紀の間続き、古代のオリンピアの聖地のスタジアムと戦車競技場で多くの素晴らしい競技者が競った。❷続けてオリンピックに勝つことで、あるいは何十年もスポーツの頂点に居続けることで伝説になった者もいた。❸ピタゴラスの弟子ミロンは、南イタリアにあったクロトンという古代ギリシャ都市の出身だったが、とりわけ有名な競技者の1人だった。❹彼は紀元前540年に第60回オリンピアードで初参加の競技で勝ち、紀元前512年第67回オリンピアードで若い競技者に最後に負けるまで勝ち続け、6回もオリンピックのレスリングの優勝者の冠を授けられた。❺ロドス島のレオニダス（紀元前164–152年）も4回連続のオリンピアードでそれぞれ3つのレースに勝って名声を得て、全部で12のオリンピックの勝利の冠を獲得した。❻彼は同郷人に英雄として称賛された。

6 ❶古代オリンピックは、キリスト教徒であるローマ帝国皇帝テオドシウス1世が異教の影響を理由に廃止する西暦393年まで1,200年近く続いた。❷1,500年以上途絶えた後、ギリシャのエバンゲリス・ザッパス、英国のウィリアム・ブルックス、フランスのピエール・ド・クーベルタンという3人の重要人物によってオリンピックの理念が復活されるきっかけになった。❸ザッパスとブルックスは互いに知り合いではなかったが、古典文学の熱狂者として、近代オリンピックを求めて訴えたデミトリス・スーツォスという名のギリシャの詩人を称賛し、この訴えこそが2人に別々に独自の大会を開始させたのだった。❹ザッパスは、一財産築いた後にその富を使って1859年からアテネにおける一連のオリンピアードの初回大会に資金提供した起業家だった。❺その間、ブルックスは英国のシュロップシャーのマッチ・ウェンロックの小さな町で彼独自の大会を始めた。❻1887年までには、これらは進化して英国オリンピックになった。❼彼の大会は女性初の競技を見せたことでとくに注目に値するものだった。❽1881年、ブルックスはギリシャ政府に、シュロップシャーとアテネの似たような試合を国際化するように提案した。❾この考えをド・クーベルタンが取り上げ、彼は1896年パリに始まる真に国際的な行事の初回大会を組織することに尽力した。

☐ truce	〔名〕停戦
☐ secular	〔形〕世俗的な、非宗教的な
☐ regardless of ...	〔熟〕…に関係なく
☐ be entitled to ...	〔熟〕…する権利が与えられる
☐ martial	〔形〕好戦的な
☐ consecutive	〔形〕連続した
☐ acclaim O as …	〔熟〕O を…として称賛する
☐ pagan	〔形〕異教徒の
☐ languish	〔動〕不振である
☐ momentum	〔名〕勢い、はずみ

正解一覧

14 C	**15** C	**16** A	**17** D	**18** D
19 truce	**20** relations	**21** weights	**22** pankration	
23 Christian	**24** D	**25** A	**26** B	

問題文和訳

Questions 14–18

正しいものを A, B, C, D から選びなさい。

解答用紙の 14–18 の欄に解答を記入しなさい。

14 本文によれば、古代オリンピックの試合で競う資格がないのは下記のどれか。

A 未婚のギリシャ人農夫

B ペロポネソスの男性市民

C ギリシャ人奴隷

D ギリシャ人民兵の一員

15 古代の公式の授賞式ではどんな賞が授与されたか。

A オリンピック・メダル

B 赤いリボン

C オリーブの冠

D 花輪

16 古代の競技では馬術の種目として何が含まれていたか。
- **A** 戦車レース
- **B** 五種競技
- **C** 槍投げ
- **D** 円盤投げ

17 ミロンは非常に有名だった理由は何か。
- **A** 最初のオリンピックのレスリングのチャンピオンだった
- **B** 第67回オリンピックで6つの栄冠を勝ち取った
- **C** 最も多くの栄冠を勝ち取った
- **D** 同じ競技で長期間勝利した

18 近代オリンピックはいつ国際的な地位を得たか。
- **A** 1859
- **B** 1887
- **C** 1881
- **D** 1896

14 |正解| C
2段落1文に古代オリンピックに参加する資格があったのはAll free male Greek citizens（ギリシャの自由市民の男性全員）と明記されていることから、奴隷に参加権がないことがわかる。

15 |正解| C
公式の授賞式については2段落5文以降に記述があるが、6文に a sacred olive tree wreath would be placed on the winner's head（勝者の頭に聖なるオリーブの木の冠をのせた）とある。

16 |正解| A
馬が必要な競技として4段落6文にchariot races（戦車レース）について言及されている。

17 |正解| D
ミロンについては5段落に言及されているが、4文のHe was crowned Olympic wrestling champion no fewer than six times（6回もオリンピックのレスリングの優勝者の冠を授けられた）という記述から、彼が長期間に渡り同じ種目で勝ち続けたといえる。

18 |正解| D
6段落の終わりにthe first truly international events that began in Paris in

1896（1896年パリに始まる真に国際的な行事の初回大会）とある。

問題文和訳

Questions 19–23

本文から1語だけを選んで下の文を完成しなさい。

解答用紙の19–23の解答欄に解答を記入しなさい。

19 競技者と市民の安全を守るため大会の間は<u>休戦</u>が必要だった。

20 アスリートの身体能力を披露させることに加えて、古代の競技会はギリシャの様々な地域間の<u>関係</u>を促進するために企画されていた。

21 古代の競技会から競技種目の多くには変更が加えられていないが、今では競技者は飛距離を伸ばすために<u>重り</u>を持たない。

22 古代の競技会における最も過激な格闘技は<u>パンクラティオン</u>であった。

23 <u>キリスト教徒</u>のローマ皇帝が宗教的理由で4世紀に競技会を中止した。

19 正解 truce

1段落3文に競技者や市民の安全確保に必要なものとして休戦が挙げられている。

20 正解 relations

1段落5文に同様の記述がある。本文中のas well as（〜同様に）と設問文中のin addition to（〜に加えて）はどちらも2つのものを並列する役割。

21 正解 weights

3段落4文に記述がある。本文中のholding ontoは設問文中のcarryと同意。

22 正解 pankration

4段落4文に最もきつい形態の決闘としてパンクラティオンが言及されている。

23 正解 Christian

古代オリンピックを廃止したローマ皇帝については6段落1文に記述があり、キリスト教徒だったとある。

問題文和訳

Questions 24–26

下記のA–Fから正しい結末を選んでそれぞれの文を完成しなさい。

解答用紙の解答欄24–26にA–Eの正しい文字を記入しなさい。

24 レスリングとボクシングは高く評価されたのは…からだ

25 古代ギリシャの馬術競技は

26 イギリスのオリンピック大会は

　A　馬術競技場で行なわれた

　B　初めて女性の競技を導入した

　C　テセウスによって創設されたと信じられていた

　D　重要な軍事技術として発展した

　E　12世紀の間途切れず続けられた

24 |正解| D

4段落2文にWrestling was highly valued as a form of military exercise（レスリングは軍事演習の形として非常に重んじられた）とある。

25 |正解| A

4段落6文に equestrian events（馬術競技）についての記述があり、an open arena known as a hippodrome（戦車競技場として知られる屋外の場所）で行われたとある。

26 |正解| B

英国オリンピックについて、6段落7文にnoteworthy for exhibiting the first women's Olympic event（女性初の競技を見せたことで注目に値する）ものだったとある。

オオカミの帰還

1 ❶かつて至るところにいたオオカミがヨーロッパ、北アメリカの多くの地域でほぼ絶滅するまで狩りつくされてしまった。❷何世紀にも渡ってオオカミは危険な害獣だと考えられ、殺すことがハンターにとって賞金稼ぎの良い方法になることも多かった。❸中世の英国の王たちは受取人がオオカミ狩りを実行することを条件に、公有地の供与さえしたものだった。❹西ヨーロッパでは、人口が拡大するにつれて、人々が森林を伐採し、オオカミの食糧となる動物を食べたので、オオカミは生息地の縮小に直面した。❺結果として、イタリアとスペインに少数が残ったものの、西ヨーロッパのほぼ全域からオオカミは消えた。

2 ❶アメリカ合衆国では、入植者がジェームズタウンに居住を確立したほぼその瞬間から、彼らの家畜を食べ始めた数多くのオオカミを根絶しようとイギリス人開拓者達が尽力した。❷こうした取り組みはエスカレートして、1850年代にはユタ州がオオカミを殺すことに予算の10%以上をかけていた。❸しかし、あらゆるおとぎ話にはハッピーエンドがあり、あかずきんのような子供の訓話でよく悪者を演じて恐怖そのものであった動物が復帰を果たしている。❹大きな悪者の人類は自らのやり方の間違いを理解するようになり、今オオカミを殺すよりもむしろ保護しようとしている。

3 ❶このような方向転換は、ひとつには田舎の人口減少につながる、田舎から都会への長期に渡る人口移動によって生じた。❷同時に、各国政府が木材を得るためにかつて森林開発を行った地域に木々を植え始めているので、森林地帯が再び拡がり始めている。❸さらに、鹿やイノシシのような野生動物の狩りをする人たちが最近ほとんどいないので、これらの動物の個体数が増加している。❹こうしたすべての傾向が環境をオオカミの帰還にふさわしくするのに役立っている。

4 ❶オオカミに対する人々の姿勢も変化している。❷19世紀や20世紀の初期、環境保護主義者達は捕食動物が餌とする動物達を保護するために、オオカミや他の捕食動物を殺すことは正当化されると信じていた。❸しかし、アメリカの環境保護運動の影響力のある人物であるアルド・レオポルドは反対した。❹以前はオオカミが抑制していたが増え続けている鹿や他の餌動物が森林の小さな木々や若木を食べ尽くすだろうから、ある地域からオオカミが消滅するとその地域が悪化することがよくあると彼は指摘した。

5 ❶田舎から都市への人々の移動はオオカミのロマンチックなイメージをかきたてることにもつながり、今では危険な殺し屋ではなく、荒野の魅力的な象徴として見なされている。❷ある意味で、オオカミが長い間悪者扱いされてきたのは不思議だ。❸クマはもっと危険で動揺すると攻撃することがあるのに対して、オオカミはたいてい逃げる。❹人々の姿勢が変化したことは、ヨーロッパの多くの国々と北アメリカのオオカミを含む、危機に瀕している種の絶滅を防ぐ法律の制定にもつながっている。

6 ❶ヨーロッパでは、1977年フィンランドからスウェーデンへ、1992年イタリアからフランスへ、1990年代に始まった20年の期間でポーランドからドイツ、オランダ、ベルギーへと国境を越え、オオカミは自発的に帰還している。❷ヨーロッパでは、オオカミはEUの生息地指令からの保護を受けている。❸しかし、オオカミが人口集中地域に移動するにつれて、お馴染みの問題が再びぶり返してきている。❹約160頭のオオカミが暮らすドイツ、ブランデンブルグの田舎で、オオカミがここ6年で360頭の羊を殺している。❺地元政府はその損失を農夫に補償するための基金を設立したが、補償金を要求することは時間のかかる役所仕事的な作業だ。❻さらに、狩猟を成功しやすくするために大きな群れで移動する北アメリカのオオカミと違って、ドイツのオオカミの群れはたいてい親と子から成り、こうした小さな家族は他の場所で食糧が乏しい時に食糧を探し求めて小さな町に迷い込んでくる傾向がある。

7 ❶西ヨーロッパのほとんどでオオカミの数が増えているが、北アメリカでは個体数の増加が劇的で、動物保護法と少ない人口が相まってオオカミは恩恵を受けている。❷例えばロシアのような国々からオオカミが長距離移動する西ヨーロッパと違って、アメリカ合州国政府は積極的にオオカミをいくつかの地域に再導入している。❸1995年、14頭のハイイロオオカミがカナダで捕獲され、イエローストーン国立公園とアイダホ近くで放されたが、そこですぐに繁殖して生態系に劇的な影響を及ぼしている。❹この導入以来、イエローストーンのヘラジカの個体数は約2万から5千に減少し、多くの草食動物がいなくなったため、特に若い柳とアスペンの木々などの草木が繁茂し、成木になることが可能になっている。❺バイソンとビーバーも新たな生息地で繁殖し、オオカミが殺す獲物をあさるグリズリーも順調だ。

8 ❶しかし、すべての人がオオカミの帰還を支持しているわけではない。❷ヨーロッパのようにアメリカの農夫も損害に苦しみ、オオカミの近くで生活する牛が不安になると、平均体重の低下につながる。❸現在オオカミの数が回復したので、ある地域では保護が外され、ロッキー山脈、五大湖周辺の全ての州でオオカミの狩猟が可能だ。❹問題は数のバランスをとることで、そうすれば畜産農家、環境、オオカミが一緒に繁栄する

ことが可能になる。

- [ ] **grant** 〔名〕助成金
- [ ] **on condition that ...** 〔熟〕…を条件に
- [ ] **wipe out** 〔動〕一掃する（絶滅させる）
- [ ] **budget** 〔名〕予算
- [ ] **come about** 〔動〕生じる
- [ ] **prey** 〔名〕餌食、餌動物
- [ ] **keep O in check** 〔熟〕O を抑制する
- [ ] **legislation** 〔名〕法律制定
- [ ] **bureaucratic** 〔形〕官僚の
- [ ] **scavenge …** 〔動〕（ごみ、残飯などを）あさる

正解一覧

27 NOT GIVEN	**28** FALSE	**29** NOT GIVEN
30 FALSE	**31** TRUE	**32** TRUE
33 TRUE	**34** bounties	**35** habitats
36 livestock	**37** endangered	**38** reintroduced
39 maturity	**40** compensation	

問題文和訳

Questions 27–33

以下の文は本文に与えられた情報と一致するか？
解答用紙の解答欄 27–33 に…を書きなさい。

TRUE もし文が情報と一致すれば

FALSE もし文が情報に矛盾すれば

NOT GIVEN もしこれについての情報がなければ

27 英国の王は昔オオカミの表皮1枚1枚に対して報酬を出した。

28 しばらくの間、どのヨーロッパの国にもオオカミはいなかった。

29 アメリカに渡った英国人入植者はすぐに地元のオオカミを一掃した。

30 環境保護論者のレオポルドはオオカミを殺すことは正当化されると考え

た。

31 ドイツでは、死んだ羊に対する補償金を得ることは難しいと農夫は感じる。

32 イエローストーンのヘラジカの数は1995年以来著しく減少している。

33 オオカミが近くにいると家畜はストレスに苦しむ。

27 |正解| NOT GIVEN

1段落3文にオオカミの狩猟でland grants（公有地）の供与を行なったという記述はあるが、表皮に対する報酬という記述はない。

28 |正解| FALSE

1段落5文に「西ヨーロッパのほぼ全域から消えた」とあるが、さらに「イタリアとスペインに少数が残った」とあるのでゼロになった時期はない。

29 |正解| NOT GIVEN

2段落1文に「根絶しようと尽力した」とあるが、実際に一掃したという情報はない。

30 |正解| FALSE

4段落2文でオオカミを殺すことに対して「19世紀や20世紀の初期、環境保護主義者達は正当化されると考えた」とあるが、3文に「レオポルドは反対した」とあるので誤り。

31 |正解| TRUE

6段落5文で、補償金に対して「基金は設立したが、要求は時間のかかる役所仕事的な作業」という趣旨の記述があるので正しい。

32 |正解| TRUE

ヘラジカに関して、7段落3～4文で「1995年のハイイロオオカミの導入以来、2万から5千に減った」ことが述べられているので正しい。

33 |正解| TRUE

8段落2文で「周辺にオオカミがいるとその不安から牛の体重が落ちる」という趣旨の記述があるので正しい。

▌問題文和訳

Questions 34–40

以下の要約を完成させなさい。

それぞれの解答を本文から1語で選びなさい。

解答用紙の解答欄34–40に解答を記入しなさい。

<h2 style="text-align:center">オオカミの帰還</h2>

その昔、オオカミはヨーロッパ中に生息して害獣とみなされていた。その結果、オオカミは頻繁に**34** 懸賞金 をかけられた。狼狩りに加え、人口の増加に対抗せねばならず、徐々にその**35** 生息地 を縮小していった。アメリカ合衆国では、オオカミは入植者の**36** 家畜 を脅かすため容赦なく狩猟された。しかし、田舎から都市への人間の移動に加え、オオカミは自然環境に利益をもたらすという認識が人々の姿勢の変化につながり、現在西ヨーロッパとアメリカ両方の政府がオオカミを含む **37** 絶滅危惧 種を保護する法律を可決した。その結果としてオオカミはヨーロッパの多くに国々に帰還を始めたが、アメリカのイエローストーン国立公園では オオカミは**38** 再導入 されなければならなかった。こうした変化は、とりわけヘラジカの数が減少し木々が**39** 成木 まで育つようになったイエロー公園で非常に有益であることがわかった。しかし、地方自治体から **40** 補償金 を受け取るための申請が可能なものの、農夫は家畜の損害を受け入れなければならない。

34 |正解| bounties

1段落2文にオオカミ狩りがa good way for hunters to earn bounties（ハンターにおいて賞金稼ぎの良い方法）とある。

35 |正解| habitats

1段落4文にshrinking habitats（生息地の縮小）とある。shrink とreduce は同意である。

36 |正解| livestock

2段落1文にwolves that began feasting on their livestock（彼らの家畜を食べ始めたオオカミ）とあり、「入植者の家畜を脅かす」とすると同じ内容の要約文になる。

37 |正解| endangered

5段落4文にlegislation preventing the extinction of endangered species, which have often included the wolf（オオカミを含む、危機に瀕している種の絶滅を防ぐ法律）の制定につながったとある。endangered species と endangered animals は同意ととらえられる。

38 |正解| reintroduced

7段落2文にthe U.S. government has actively reintroduced wolves to some areas（アメリカ合州国政府は積極的にオオカミをいくつかの地域に再導入している）とある。

39 |正解| maturity

7段落4文でヘラジカの減少による柳やポプラの木の繁殖について説明され

ている。maturityは「成熟」の意味。成熟した木々を指すため「成木」と訳
してある。

40 ‖正解‖ **compensation**

6段落5文にclaiming compensation（補償金を要求すること）に言及があ
る。要約文中のapplying for compensationと同意である。

Exercise 01

DATE _____

The Hidden Strengths of the Introvert

該当番号のAnswer枠内に解答を記入しなさい。自信がない場合はunsureのボックスにチェックをつけて解答しなさい。

	Answer	unsure
1		☐
2		☐
3		☐
4		☐
5		☐
6		☐
7		☐
8		☐
9		☐
10		☐
11		☐
12		☐
13		☐
14		☐

TOTAL

解答上の注意

・解答は全て鉛筆でハッキリと記入すること。

・解答枠からはみ出さないように記入すること。

・スペリングミスのないように確認すること。

採点上の注意

・スペリングミス、解答枠からはみ出た解答、読みづらい、または不明瞭な解答は失点とする。

・unsure（あいまい）にマークを付けたものは、必ず解答解説で正解の理由を確認すること。

Exercise 02

DATE _____

Cities of the Future

該当番号のAnswer枠内に解答を記入しなさい。自信がない場合はunsureのボックスにチェックをつけて解答しなさい。

	Answer	unsure
1		☐
2		☐
3		☐
4		☐
5		☐
6		☐
7		☐
8		☐
9		☐
10		☐
11		☐
12		☐
13		☐

TOTAL [ ]

解答上の注意

・解答は全て鉛筆でハッキリと記入すること。

・解答枠からはみ出さないように記入すること。

・スペリングミスのないように確認すること。

採点上の注意

・スペリングミス、解答枠からはみ出た解答、読みづらい、または不明瞭な解答は失点とする。

・unsure（あいまい）にマークを付けたものは、必ず解答解説で正解の理由を確認すること。

Exercise 03

The Life of Isaac Newton

該当番号のAnswer枠内に解答を記入しなさい。自信がない場合はunsureのボックスにチェックをつけて解答しなさい。

	Answer	unsure
1		☐
2		☐
3		☐
4		☐
5		☐
6		☐
7		☐
8		☐
9		☐
10		☐
11		☐
12		☐
13		☐

TOTAL	

解答上の注意

・解答は全て鉛筆でハッキリと記入すること。

・解答枠からはみ出さないように記入すること。

・スペリングミスのないように確認すること。

採点上の注意

・スペリングミス、解答枠からはみ出た解答、読みづらい、または不明瞭な解答は失点とする。

・unsure（あいまい）にマークを付けたものは、必ず解答解説で正解の理由を確認すること。

Exercise 04

DATE _____

The Gaia Theory

該当番号のAnswer枠内に解答を記入しなさい。自信がない場合はunsureのボックスにチェックをつけて解答しなさい。

	Answer	unsure
1		☐
2		☐
3		☐
4		☐
5		☐
6		☐
7		☐
8		☐
9		☐
10		☐
11		☐
12		☐
13		☐

TOTAL

解答上の注意

・解答は全て鉛筆でハッキリと記入すること。

・解答枠からはみ出さないように記入すること。

・スペリングミスのないように確認すること。

採点上の注意

・スペリングミス、解答枠からはみ出た解答、読みづらい、または不明瞭な解答は失点とする。

・unsure（あいまい）にマークを付けたものは、必ず解答解説で正解の理由を確認すること。

DATE _____

The Mediterranean Diet

該当番号のAnswer枠内に解答を記入しなさい。自信がない場合はunsureのボックスにチェックをつけて解答しなさい。

	Answer	unsure
1		☐
2		☐
3		☐
4		☐
5		☐
6		☐
7		☐
8		☐
9		☐
10		☐
11		☐
12		☐
13		☐

TOTAL

解答上の注意
・解答は全て鉛筆でハッキリと記入すること。
・解答枠からはみ出さないように記入すること。
・スペリングミスのないように確認すること。

採点上の注意
・スペリングミス、解答枠からはみ出た解答、読みづらい、または不明瞭な解答は失点とする。
・unsure（あいまい）にマークを付けたものは、必ず解答解説で正解の理由を確認すること。

Exercise 06

DATE _____

The Coffee House

該当番号のAnswer枠内に解答を記入しなさい。自信がない場合はunsureのボックスにチェックをつけて解答しなさい。

	Answer	unsure
1		☐
2		☐
3		☐
4		☐
5		☐
6		☐
7		☐
8		☐
9		☐
10		☐
11		☐
12		☐
13		☐

TOTAL

解答上の注意

・解答は全て鉛筆でハッキリと記入すること。

・解答枠からはみ出さないように記入すること。

・スペリングミスのないように確認すること。

採点上の注意

・スペリングミス、解答枠からはみ出た解答、読みづらい、または不明瞭な解答は失点とする。

・unsure（あいまい）にマークを付けたものは、必ず解答解説で正解の理由を確認すること。

Exercise 07

3D Printing : The Next Industrial Revolution

該当番号のAnswer枠内に解答を記入しなさい。自信がない場合はunsureのボックスにチェックをつけて解答しなさい。

	Answer	unsure
1		☐
2		☐
3		☐
4		☐
5		☐
6		☐
7		☐
8		☐
9		☐
10		☐
11		☐
12		☐
13		☐

TOTAL

解答上の注意

・解答は全て鉛筆でハッキリと記入すること。

・解答枠からはみ出さないように記入すること。

・スペリングミスのないように確認すること。

採点上の注意

・スペリングミス、解答枠からはみ出た解答、読みづらい、または不明瞭な解答は失点とする。

・unsure（あいまい）にマークを付けたものは、必ず解答解説で正解の理由を確認すること。

Farm fish but not farm fresh

該当番号のAnswer枠内に解答を記入しなさい。自信がない場合はunsureのボックスにチェックをつけて解答しなさい。

	Answer	unsure
1		☐
2		☐
3		☐
4		☐
5		☐
6		☐
7		☐
8		☐
9		☐
10		☐
11		☐
12		☐
13		☐

TOTAL

解答上の注意
・解答は全て鉛筆でハッキリと記入すること。
・解答枠からはみ出さないように記入すること。
・スペリングミスのないように確認すること。

採点上の注意
・スペリングミス、解答枠からはみ出た解答、読みづらい、または不明瞭な解答は失点とする。
・unsure（あいまい）にマークを付けたものは、必ず解答解説で正解の理由を確認すること。

Out of Africa

該当番号のAnswer枠内に解答を記入しなさい。自信がない場合はunsureのボックスにチェックをつけて解答しなさい。

	Answer	unsure
1		☐
2		☐
3		☐
4		☐
5		☐
6		☐
7		☐
8		☐
9		☐
10		☐
11		☐
12		☐
13		☐

TOTAL	

解答上の注意

・解答は全て鉛筆でハッキリと記入すること。

・解答枠からはみ出さないように記入すること。

・スペリングミスのないように確認すること。

採点上の注意

・スペリングミス、解答枠からはみ出た解答、読みづらい、または不明瞭な解答は失点とする。

・unsure（あいまい）にマークを付けたものは、必ず解答解説で正解の理由を確認すること。

A Question of Life and Death

該当番号のAnswer枠内に解答を記入しなさい。自信がない場合はunsureのボックスにチェックをつけて解答しなさい。

	Answer	unsure
1		☐
2		☐
3		☐
4		☐
5		☐
6		☐
7		☐
8		☐
9		☐
10		☐
11		☐
12		☐
13		☐

TOTAL

解答上の注意
・解答は全て鉛筆でハッキリと記入すること。
・解答枠からはみ出さないように記入すること。
・スペリングミスのないように確認すること。

採点上の注意
・スペリングミス、解答枠からはみ出た解答、読みづらい、または不明瞭な解答は失点とする。
・unsure（あいまい）にマークを付けたものは、必ず解答解説で正解の理由を確認すること。

Keynes vs Hayek : The Economic Fight of the Century

該当番号のAnswer枠内に解答を記入しなさい。自信がない場合はunsureのボックスにチェックをつけて解答しなさい。

	Answer	unsure
1		☐
2		☐
3		☐
4		☐
5		☐
6		☐
7		☐
8		☐
9		☐
10		☐
11		☐
12		☐
13		☐

	TOTAL	

解答上の注意

・解答は全て鉛筆でハッキリと記入すること。

・解答枠からはみ出さないように記入すること。

・スペリングミスのないように確認すること。

採点上の注意

・スペリングミス、解答枠からはみ出た解答、読みづらい、または不明瞭な解答は失点とする。

・unsure（あいまい）にマークを付けたものは、必ず解答解説で正解の理由を確認すること。

Learning in the East and West

該当番号のAnswer枠内に解答を記入しなさい。自信がない場合はunsureのボックスにチェックをつけて解答しなさい。

	Answer	unsure
1		☐
2		☐
3		☐
4		☐
5		☐
6		☐
7		☐
8		☐
9		☐
10		☐
11		☐
12		☐
13		☐

TOTAL [ ]

解答上の注意

・解答は全て鉛筆でハッキリと記入すること。

・解答枠からはみ出さないように記入すること。

・スペリングミスのないように確認すること。

採点上の注意

・スペリングミス、解答枠からはみ出た解答、読みづらい、または不明瞭な解答は失点とする。

・unsure（あいまい）にマークを付けたものは、必ず解答解説で正解の理由を確認すること。

実戦模試

Reading Reading Reading Reading Reading

該当番号のAnswer枠内に解答を記入しなさい。自信がない場合はunsureのボックスにチェックをつけて解答しなさい。

解答時間：60分

	Answer	unsure
1		☐
2		☐
3		☐
4		☐
5		☐
6		☐
7		☐
8		☐
9		☐
10		☐
11		☐
12		☐
13		☐
14		☐
15		☐
16		☐
17		☐
18		☐
19		☐
20		☐
21		☐

22		☐
23		☐
24		☐
25		☐
26		☐
27		☐
28		☐
29		☐
30		☐
31		☐
32		☐
33		☐
34		☐
35		☐
36		☐
37		☐
38		☐
39		☐
40		☐

TOTAL

解答上の注意

・解答は全て鉛筆でハッキリと記入すること。

・解答枠からはみ出さないように記入すること。

・スペリングミスのないように確認すること。

採点上の注意

・スペリングミス、解答枠からはみ出た解答、読みづらい、または不明瞭な解答は失点とする。

・unsure（あいまい）にマークを付けたものは、必ず解答解説で正解の理由を確認すること。

［編著者紹介］

トフルゼミナール
1979 年に英米留学専門予備校として設立以来 IELTS、TOEFL、SAT、GRE、GMAT など海
外留学のための英語資格試験対策や渡航準備などを通し、多くの海外留学をめざす学習者をサ
ポート。国内大学受験においては、東京外国語大学、早稲田大学国際教養学部、上智大学国際教養
学部、国際基督教大学（ICU）など英語重視難関校対策や、AO・推薦入試のための英語資格試験
対策、エッセイ指導等を行なっている。

執筆協力：一ノ瀬安、Geoff Tozer、鶴田 博美、小沢芳、Guenter Brook
編集協力：徳永和博
DTP：有限会社中央制作社

パーフェクト攻略 IELTS リーディング 新装版

発行	：2017 年 3 月 30 日　第 1 版第 1 刷
	2024 年 4 月 20 日　新装版第 4 刷
著者	：トフルゼミナール
発行者	：山内哲夫
企画・編集	：トフルゼミナール英語教育研究所
発行所	：テイエス企画株式会社
	〒 169-0075　東京都新宿区高田馬場 1-30-5 千寿ビル 6F
	E-mail　books@tseminar.co.jp
	URL　https://www.tofl.jp/books/
印刷・製本	：シナノ書籍印刷株式会社